Art of Our Time

Art
of Our Time

The Saatchi Collection

Lund Humphries London

in association with

Art of Our Time

Copyright © 1984 Lund Humphries Publishers Ltd

Published in 1984
(except in the United States of America) by
Lund Humphries Publishers Ltd
26 Litchfield Street   London WC2H 9NJ

ISBN 0 85331 478 0   paperback
ISBN 0 85331 482 9   casebound in boxed set of 4
volumes

Published in 1985 in the United States of America by
Rizzoli International Publications Inc
712 Fifth Avenue   New York NY 10019

ISBN 0–8478–0576–X   paperback

LC 84–61639

Designed by Herbert & Mafalda Spencer
Made and printed in Great Britain by
Lund Humphries Printers, London and Bradford

Published in four volumes:

Book 1

ANDRE BAER BELL FLAVIN HESSE JUDD LEWITT MANGOLD MARDEN MARTIN McCRACKEN MORRIS NAUMAN RYMAN SANDBACK SERRA TUTTLE

By Peter Schjeldahl

Book 2

ARTSCHWAGER CHAMBERLAIN SAMARAS STELLA TWOMBLY WARHOL

By Jean-Christophe Ammann Michael Auping Robert Rosenblum Peter Schjeldahl

Book 3

BASELITZ GUSTON KIEFER MORLEY POLKE SCHNABEL

By Rudi Fuchs Hilton Kramer Peter Schjeldahl

Book 4

BARTLETT BOROFSKY BURTON CLOSE FISCHL GOLUB JENNEY JENSEN LONGO MURRAY NUTT ROTHENBERG SALLE SHAPIRO SHERMAN WINTERS

By Prudence Carlson Lynne Cooke Hilton Kramer Kim Levin Mark Rosenthal Phyllis Tuchman

CLEMENTE

By Michael Auping

DEACON HODGKIN KOSSOFF SCULLY WILLING

By Lynne Cooke

List of Illustrations

Dimensions are given first in inches, then in centimetres.
Height precedes width precedes depth, unless otherwise indicated.

GEORG BASELITZ

1
Partisan
1965
Oil on canvas
64×52 (162×132)

2
MMM in G und A
1961/62/66
Oil on canvas
78×58 (195×145)

3
Kullervos Füsse
1967
Oil on canvas
64×51 (162×130)

4
B. für Larry
1967
Oil on canvas
98½×79 (250×200)

5
Zwei Meissener Waldarbeiter
1967
Oil on canvas
98½×79 (250×200)

6
Graue Hunde, Drei Streifen
1967/68
Oil on canvas
64×51 (162×130)

7
Waldarbeiter
1968/69
Oil on canvas
98½×79 (250×200)

8
Waldarbeiter
1968
Oil on canvas
98½×79 (250×200)

9
Dreieck zwischen Arm und Rumpf
1977
Oil on canvas
98½×79 (250×200)

10
Akt und Flasche (diptych)
1977
Oil and tempera on wood
2 panels, Each: 98½×67 (250×170)

11
Portrait und Adler (diptych)
1978
Oil and tempera on wood
2 panels, Each: 98½×67 (250×170)

12
Die Frau in der Tür
1978
Oil and tempera on canvas
130×98½ (330×250)

13
Night in Tunisia II
1980
Oil on canvas
98½×79 (250×200)

14
Die Mädchen von Olmo
1981
Oil on canvas
98½×94½ (250×248)

15
Weg vom Fenster
1982
Oil on canvas
98½×98½ (250×250)

16
Der Trommler
1982
Oil on canvas
98½×130 (250×330)

17
Untitled
1982
Painted wood
98½×36×24 (250×90×60)

18
Die Dornenkrönung
1983
Oil on canvas
117×97½ (297·2×247·7)

19
Nachtessen in Dresden
1983
Oil on canvas
110×177 (280×450)

PHILIP GUSTON

20
Head, Bottle, Light
1969
Oil on canvas
20×22 (50·8×55·9)

21
Painter in Bed
1973
Oil on canvas
60×104 (152·4×264·2)

22
The Magnet
1975
Oil on canvas
67½×80½ (171·5×204·5)

23
Frame
1976
Oil on canvas
74×116 (188×294·6)

24
Rug III
1976
Oil on canvas
69×110½ (175·3×280·7)

25
Edge
1976
Oil on canvas
80×124¾ (203·3×316·9)

26
Friend – to M.F.
1978
Oil on canvas
68×88 (172·7×223·5)

ANSELM KIEFER

27
Maikäfer flieg
1974
Oil on burlap
86⅝×118 (220×300)

28
Bilderstreit
1976/77
Oil on canvas
128×130 (325×330)

29
Wege der Weltweisheit: die Hermannsschlacht
1978
Woodcut in 31 parts on blotting and handmade paper, acrylic and shellac
133⁷⁄₈×137³⁄₄ (340×350)

30
Baum mit Palette
1978
Oil on canvas with lead object
114¼×73 (290×185)

31
Noch ist Polen nicht verloren IV
1978
Oil on canvas
75×112 (190×285)

32
Wege der Weltweisheit: die Hermannsschlacht
1978
Woodcut in several parts on blotting and handmade paper, emulsion, acrylic, and shellac on canvas
114¼×78³⁄₄ (290×200)

33
Wege: märkischer Sand
1980
Oil, emulsion, shellac, sand, photograph (on projection paper) on canvas
110×150 (280×380)

34
Wege: märkischer Sand
1980
Acrylic, sand, photograph (on projection paper) on burlap
100½×141³⁄₄ (255×360)

35
Palette am Seil
1981
Oil and acrylic on canvas
82⁵⁄₈×128 (210×320)

36
Ikarus=Märkischer Sand
1981
Oil, emulsion, shellac, sand, photograph (on projection paper) on canvas
114¼×141³⁄₄ (290×360)

37
Dein blondes Haar, Margarete (diptych)
1981
Oil and straw on canvas
Each panel: 46½×86 (118×218)
Overall: 46½×177 (118×449·6)

38
Die drei Nornen (Urd Werdandi Skuld)
1981
Oil on canvas
66×75 (168×190)

39
Die Meistersinger
1981
Oil, acrylic, straw on canvas
73×130 (185×330)

40
Margarethe
1981
Oil and straw on canvas
110×150 (280×380)

41
Gilgamesch im Zedernwald
1981/82
Oil and straw on canvas
78³⁄₄×114¼ (200×290)

42
Die Meistersinger
1982
Oil, acrylic, straw and cardboard on canvas
110×150 (280×380)

43
Wölundlied
1982
Oil, emulsion, straw, photograph (on projection paper) on canvas with lead wing
110×150 (280×380)

44
Wölundlied
1982
Oil, emulsion, straw, photograph (on projection paper) on canvas with lead wing
110×150 (280×380)

45
Wölundlied
1982
Oil, emulsion, straw, photograph (on projection paper) on canvas with iron, wood and metal tongs
110×150 (280×380)

46
Der Rhein
1982
Woodcut in several parts on blotting and handmade paper, mounted on canvas
118×150 (300×380)

47
Heliogabal
1983
Oil, emulsion, woodcut, shellac, acrylic, and straw on canvas
110×110 (280×280)

48
Sulamith
1983
Oil, emulsion, woodcut, shellac, acrylic, and straw on canvas
114¼×145³⁄₄ (290×370)

49
Unternehmen Seelöwe
1983/84
Oil/emulsion, shellac, acrylic, straw, photograph (on projection paper) on canvas
150×218½ (380×555)

MALCOLM MORLEY

50
SS Amsterdam in front of Rotterdam
1966
Acrylic on canvas
62×84 (157·5×213·5)

51
Vermeer, Portrait of the Artist in his Studio
1968
Acrylic on canvas
105×87 (266·5×221)

52
Safety is Your Business
1971
Oil on canvas
88×110 (224×280)

53
Picasso Bridge
1972
Oil on canvas
48×66 (122×168)

54
School of Athens
1972
Oil and acrylic on canvas
67×94½ (170×240)

55
Untitled Souvenirs, Europe
1973
Oil and mixed media on canvas with objects attached
96¼×68¼ (244·5×173·3)

56
SS France
1974
Oil and mixed media on canvas with objects attached
72×64 (183×162·5)

57
Age of Catastrophe
1976
Oil on canvas
60×96 (152·5×244)

58
Out Dark Spot
1978
Oil on canvas
72⁵⁄₈×98³⁄₄ (185·3×250·8)

59
Camels and Goats
1980
Oil on canvas
66½×100 (169×254)

60
Arizonac
1981
Oil on canvas
80×105 (203×266·5)

61
Indian Winter
1981
Oil on canvas
53×77 (134·6×195·6)

62
Macaws, Bengals, with Mullet
1982
Oil on canvas
120×80 (305×203)

63
Farewell to Crete
1984
Oil on canvas
80×164 (203·2×416·6)

SIGMAR POLKE

64
Plastik-Wannen
1964
Oil on canvas
37×47¼ (94×120)

65
Liebespaar II
1965
Oil and enamel on canvas
75×55 (190×140)

66
Bunnies
1966
Oil on canvas
59×39½ (150×100)

67
Rasterbild mit Palmen
1966
Oil on canvas
52×44 (130×110)

68
Reiherbild II
1968
Dispersion on flannel
74³/₄×59 (190×150)

69
Wolldeckenbild mit kleinen weissen Quadraten
1968
Dispersion on wool blanket
59×49¹/₄ (150×125)

70
Portrait of David Lamelas (Obelisk)
1971
Dispersion and spray enamel on canvas
51×59 (130×150)

71
Ich mach das schon Jess
1972
Oil on felt
124×112 (315×285)

72
Zwei Köpfe
1971/73
Oil and cellulose on canvas
51×43 (130×110)

73
Skelett
1974
Dispersion on fabric
77×72 (196×183)

74
Affen
1974
Dispersion and spray enamel on canvas
71×59 (180×150)

75
Burda
1979/82
Dispersion on fabric
8 panels, Each: 35¹/₂×27¹/₂ (90×70)
Overall: 71×120¹/₄ (180×305)

76
Seit Benzin- und Heizölpreise fallen, wundert mich nichts mehr
1982
Dispersion on fabric
59×71 (150×180)

77
Treppenhaus
1982
Dispersion on fabric
78³/₄×177 (200×450)

78
Paganini
1982
Dispersion on canvas
78³/₄×177 (200×450)

79
Hannibal mit seinen Panzerelefanten
1982
Dispersion and lacquer on canvas
102¹/₂×79 (260×200)

80
The Copyist
1982
Dispersion and lacquer on canvas
102¹/₂×79 (260×200)

JULIAN SCHNABEL

81
No. 17 (Red Cross Painting for N. Fisher 1978)
1977/78
Oil on canvas
96×48 (240×122)

82
Accatone
1978
Oil on canvas
84×72 (210×180)

83
The Death of Fashion
1978
Oil, crockery on canvas and wood
90×120×13 (225×300×32·5)

84
Divan
1978
Oil and crockery on wood
96×96×18 (240×240×45)

85
Against Modernism (What to do with a corner in Madrid)
1979
Oil on canvas
96×96 (240×240)

86
Insomnolent Brown Trimmed in Mink
1980
Oil on canvas
96×84 (240×210)

87
Ornamental Despair (Painting for Ian Curtis)
1980
Oil on velvet
90×168 (228·6×426·7)

88
Mr Bamboo Gets an X-ray
1980
Oil on velvet
90×168 (228·6×426·7)

89
Bob's Worlds
1980
Oil, wax, crockery on wood and canvas
97¹/₂×146 (243·8×365·7)

90
Starting to Sing: Artaud (3)
1981
Oil and rustoleum on canvas
168×156 (420×390)

91
Starting to Sing: Untitled (1)
1981
Oil and rustoleum on canvas
170×216 (425×540)

92
Starting to Sing: Florence Loeb (4)
1981
Oil and rustoleum on canvas
163×112 (407·5×280)

93
Starting to Sing: Untitled (2)
1981
Oil and rustoleum on canvas
166×228 (415×570)

94
Fouffi-Nouti in Hell
1980
Oil on Chinese silk
91×85 (228×213)

95
Aorta
1981
Oil on sisal rug with wooden frame
120×168 (300×420)

96
Pre History: Glory, Honor, Privilege and Poverty
1981
Oil and antlers on pony skin
128×177 (324×450)

97
Oar: For the one who comes out to know fear
1981
Oil, crockery, car body filler paste and wood on wood
127×175×13 (318×438×32·5)

98
Painting for Alan Moss
1981
Oil on jute
108×120 (270×300)

99
The Sea
1981
Oil and crockery on wood
108×156 (274×390)

100
Angela
1982
Oil on rug batting
132×60 (330×150)

101
Olé
1982
Oil on tarpaulin
96×132 (277×335)

102
Winter (Rose garden that Jacqueline built as a girl)
1982
Oil, crockery, antler, wood and bondo on wood
108×84 (270×210)

103
Maria Callas, No. 4
1983
Oil on velvet
108×122 (274×305)

104
Balzac
1983
Bronze
199×46×46 (497·5×115×115)

105
Vito
1983
Bronze
108×28×27 (270×70×67·5)

106
Memory and the Stimulus for Memory
1983
Oil and fibreglass on canvas
116×160 (290×400)

107
A.D. (Wreath for Tennessee Williams)
1983
Oil and fibreglass on canvas
132×96 (335×244)

Biographical Notes

GEORG BASELITZ

Born (Georg Kern) in Deutschbaselitz, Saxony, East
Germany, 1938
Education:
Hochschule der bildenden Künste, East Berlin,
1956–7
Hochschule der bildenden Künste, West Berlin,
1957–64
Awarded grant to work at Villa Romana, Florence,
Italy, 1965
Professor at:
Kunstakademie, Karlsruhe, West Germany, 1977
Hochschule der bildenden Künste, Berlin, 1983
Lives and works in Derneburg, near Hildesheim,
West Germany

PHILIP GUSTON

Born in Montréal, Quebec, Canada, 1913
(Family emigrated from Odessa, Russia, ca. 1900)
Education:
Manuel Arts High School, Los Angeles, California,
1927–8
Otis Art Institute, Los Angeles, California (admitted
on scholarship), 1930
Joined the mural section of the Works Progress
Administration Federal Art Project, 1935
Recipient of Guggenheim Foundation Fellowship,
1947
Recipient of Prix de Rome, American Academy in
Rome, 1948
Moved to New York City, 1950
Recipient of Ford Foundation Grant, 1959
Recipient of Guggenheim Foundation Fellowship,
1967
Moved to Woodstock, New York, 1967
Died in Woodstock, New York, 1980

ANSELM KIEFER

Born in Donaueschingen, West Germany, 1945
Education:
Began studies in Law and French, 1965
Akademie der bildenden Künste, Freiburg, West
Germany (studied with Peter Dreher), 1966–8
Akademie der bildenden Künste, Karlsruhe, West
Germany (studied with Horst Antes), 1969
Kunstakademie, Düsseldorf, West Germany
(studied with Joseph Beuys), 1970–2
Lives and works in Hornbach/Odenwald, West
Germany

MALCOLM MORLEY

Born in Highgate, London, England, 1931
Education:
Camberwell School of Arts & Crafts, London,
1952–3
Royal College of Art, London, 1954–7
Moved to New York City, 1958
Instructor at:
State University of Ohio, Columbus, 1965–6
School of Visual Arts, New York, 1967–9
State University of New York, Stonybrook, 1972–4
German Academic Exchange Programme
(7 months), Berlin, 1977
Lives and works in New York City

SIGMAR POLKE

Born in Oels, Germany (now Olesnica, Poland),
1941
Moved to West Germany, 1953
Education:
Studied glass painting, Düsseldorf, West Germany,
1959–60
Kunstakademie, Düsseldorf, West Germany
(studied painting with Gerhard Hoehme and Karl
Otto Goetz), 1961–7
Cofounded 'Kapitalischer Realismus' (with Konrad
Fischer-Lueg and Gerhard Richter), 1963
Professor at:
Hochschule der bildenden Künste, Hamburg, West
Germany, 1970–1
Hochschule der bildenden Künste, Hamburg, West
Germany, 1977–present
Lives and works in Cologne and Hamburg, West
Germany

JULIAN SCHNABEL

Born in New York City, 1951
Education:
University of Houston, Texas, 1969–72 (BFA)
Independent Study Program, The Whitney Museum
of American Art, New York, 1973–4
Lives and works in New York City

Rudi Fuchs   **Georg Baselitz**

Among these paintings, covering twenty years of the art of the painter Baselitz and twenty years of versatile artistic intelligence and brilliance, is one sculpture. It is a huge, heavy form, the classic figure of the erect male, proud and defiant, cut and hewn from inside a tree-trunk with the aid of saw and axe, its face painted like some ancient warrior. The sculpture is not, in the pure sense of the word, refined. Form and stance have not been developed, not directly at least, in accordance with contemporary concerns in sculpture. The piece is closely related to Baselitz's painting; both its character and its appearance are indicators to intentions in the paintings. The relevance of Baselitz's painting to sculpture is that the figure, uncompromising and forceful, *confronts* sculpture – confronts it with pictorial intelligence just as, once, the sculpture of Donatello confronted and reinforced, with its extraordinary tightness in design and proportion, the painting of his time (a fact well-observed by Alberti, I believe, when he dedicated his treatise on painting to 'my friend Donato').

Baselitz carved his first sculpture for his show at the Venice Biennale in 1980. He wanted to show it in the company of four paintings; then he decided to omit the paintings. But it was not just, I believe, this occasion which gave birth to the sculpture. There were other, internal and artistic reasons which necessitated the sculpture (and the ones immediately following it, like plate 17) – and the fact that in Venice he left out the paintings proves, I think, my point. Baselitz does not see himself as just a painter who produces paintings. In his rare interviews and also in the early manifestoes (1961), one senses his wish to be dramatic. His conception of what it means to be an artist is not someone who pleases by painting elegant paintings but someone who cuts, so to speak, into the flesh, who makes art which is deeply controversial, even brutal. It is a grand attitude of absolute aesthetic independence which is at the heart of his artistic being, which permeates his paintings, and which dictates changes in their development. He was convinced, quite early in his career, that style alone meant nothing – that one had to go beyond style. Baselitz has always been extremely sensitive to the problem of being trapped by one's own aesthetic; stylistic dependence upon oneself leads to the recurrence of formal tricks and a fading away of force and drama. That, precisely, was the problem with the tachism which the young Baselitz encountered when he moved to West Berlin in the late 1950s. To oppose tachistic decadence and narcissism he returned (as was then said) to the figure.

When the first great American exhibition was touring Berlin and other European cities (among its treasures were some extraordinary paintings by Jackson Pollock) Baselitz moved towards figurative art with a series of male 'heroes' exemplifying the New Type. For Baselitz the Hero-paintings were the proper response to Pollock. Moreover, the early *Heroes* and the complex paintings that followed, with dogs and cows, were already highly constructed and coldly calculated. They were designed for a certain effect. They had such an unusual *look,* compared to other paintings of the time, that their solitary quality could not be ignored nor could it be easily absorbed into period style. Their very resistance to such absorption is typical of Baselitz's artistic nature, of his instinct.

Baselitz is not a painter who proceeds by theoretical strategies and arguments.

When he paints a picture the development of form is the application of very concrete manipulations. With each motif there came a point when, in the eye of the artist, nothing more could be added and nothing was to be gained by mere continuation of the same. After a while, the heroic figures simply became boring; there just wasn't enough excitement left in painting them. The painting was in danger of becoming repetitive; it was concerned with itself, with the preservation of its style and image, and not with pushing further and pursuing its dramatic and provocative aspect. There then followed the pictures cut in the middle with the halves of the images shifted, experiments ending with the reversal of the motif in the late 1960s. Baselitz arrived at the upside-down motif to challenge his own painting, just as the *Heroes* challenged Pollock. The reversal of the motif meant a renewed dramatisation of the picture – dramatisation in the sense of Picasso's *Les Demoiselles d'Avignon,* Malevich's *Black Square* or certain pictures by Schwitters, paintings which define the highest level of artistic invention in the twentieth century. Baselitz is very aware of paintings like those, although he also refers to artists such as Rouault, Fautrier or Strindberg; he knows, however, that for him they are not the ones that present a challenge. His 'moves' take artists like Picasso, or, among his contemporaries, Frank Stella, into account. This competitive spirit makes him a great painter. The first paintings with their motif reversed were still painted in the factual style of the *Heroes:* the same colour schemes, the same handling of paint, the same type of brush-stroke. Very soon afterwards, though still reversing the motif, Baselitz became more realistic, painting upside-down nudes (male and female) in pale, cold yellow, and blue landscapes and interiors. The reversal of the motif, which liberated him from the figure and which later would lead, almost naturally, to 'very pictorial' pictures, became in these 'realistic' paintings almost oppressive and impossible. The paradox between motif and painting became, in fact, quite intolerable. They are not part of the present collection but they belong to Baselitz's boldest pictures.

It was in these 'realistic' paintings that the artist's reversal of the motif, was pushed to its extreme – to a form of painting which resembled a manifesto. In these paintings he defined his aim. After that he could enter into a more free, pictorial kind of painting. His use of colour changed. In the earlier paintings colour was tied to the articulation of form, almost in classical terms of light and shadow. In the paintings of the late 1970s the upside-down motif became more and more schematic, an almost abstract anchor to hold the picture's general composition in balance. Around this 'anchor' large, heavy masses of colour were organised. These areas of colour gave the picture its look, the motif often hardly more than a skeleton. In this period the paintings became bigger because the way in which Baselitz now used colour led to natural expansion.

It was at this point that he made the first sculpture. He sensed, I believe, a danger in colouristic expansion. The formal structure might easily evaporate into the chromatic space of a painting. The paintings would then lose the toughness he wanted them to have. The sculpture concentrated on form, on the single, powerful shape – and soon after that the paintings changed. Clearly defined figures returned, bringing new tension to the picture. At first they were separated from the now flatter fields of colour; sometimes they were drawn into them. In the most recent paintings the figures are constructed from shapes of very bright colour in such a way that form and colour are separate and at the same time each other's vehicle. This is a solution of great power and originality which once again secures Baselitz's independence from style.

Peter Schjeldahl   **Philip Guston**

When, in 1968, Philip Guston abruptly abandoned the most restrained and elegant
of all Abstract Expressionist painting styles for a mode of raucous figuration, I
hated it. It seemed a rank indecency, a profanation, a joke in the worst conceivable
taste. Gradually, over more than a decade, I was brought around to late Guston by
the better opinion of others, mainly artists I respected; at some point that I cannot
specify – maybe in my sleep – my resistance disintegrated, and the very paintings I
had abhorred started giving me surges of pleasure. In itself, this story is
insignificant and only mildly embarrassing: Anyone who has a mind changes it
now and then. But the tale seems worth telling, and for me is the token of an
atonement, because my own experience coincided so closely with that of the art
culture's reaction not just to Guston but to an epochal shift in sensibility of which
he was a prophet and a pioneer. Realising that my 'personal' feelings were *typical*
was a jolt which I hope has taught me something.

The truly personal component of my animus against late Guston was probably
fright. I was scared of the abject psychic content he had unclenched, and I was
scared *for* an idealistic sense of art, as a refuge from life's disorder, which I had
absorbed without examining. I didn't require classical elevation of all artists. On
the contrary, it was enough that a very few, Philip Guston prominently among
them, maintain it – as the existence of saintly monks is spiritual money in the bank
for a certain kind of fecklessly sinning believer. Defrocking himself in 1968, Guston
declared the faith bankrupt. No more saintliness, no more sin; only mortified
humanity and, if one could manage it somehow, painting. This was the
unwelcome, desperately courageous message for which many of us blamed the
messenger. And today it is our new scripture, to which many artists have added
gospels: late Picasso, Anselm Kiefer, Malcolm Morley, Susan Rothenberg, others.
None had a rougher time of it than Guston, because none sacrificed a greater stake
in the previous scheme of things.

Actually, Guston's art always had a certain sceptical, anxious, potentially sardonic
edge, palpable as a materialistic matter-of-factness in his great abstractions of the
1950s and 1960s. There was a closely-watched quality to his fantastically sensitive
brushstrokes (only de Kooning has better touch), as if they had been deployed in
the teeth of powerful misgivings, as if the painter, while avid for aesthetic glory,
had been hounded by a suspicion that the whole enterprise was a crock. Precisely
this air of haunted compunction made Guston a hero. He appeared to deal with a
level of doubt that would paralyse anyone else, and in so doing he provided
vicarious reassurance. The paradigm of high, formal, abstract painting, so
severely tested, was seen to hold, to be a fitting vessel for transcendent meanings
even amid the contrary insinuations of Pop and Minimalism and the failing
convictions of one abstractionist after another. Had Guston simply failed, there
would have been no scandal. His offence was to jettison principles that seemed
still sound – though obviously, in hindsight, they were sick unto death.

Looking today at the first late Gustons – for instance, *Head, Bottle, Light* (plate 20) –
I must squint to see them in the pejorative way I used to. That is, I must blur my
recognition of the images in order to behold an incoherent abstraction, one in
which 'arbitrary' (as I put it then) cartoonish contours generate no formal tension

with the framing edge and in which a still ravishing brushwork is demoted to the busy work of filling-in. I could not take seriously Guston's reversal of the modernist priority – the subordination of every element to an aesthetic unity – so I got his work backward, failing to see the purposes of its disunity. Now my eye surrenders to the fierce particularity of the images within the generalised container of the picture: *this* head, *this* bottle, *this* light – but only *that* painting (just another painting). The clunkiness of the composition jars the images loose and dumps them into the viewer's lap. The apparent crudity of the drawing authenticates each image as literally *drawn* – extruded by imagination from the shambling contingency of the painting process.

Painting's loss, then, is imagination's gain. (And there is a revived, if humbler, role in the world for painting.) One is not to bother with how the work was done and only in a casual way with how it looks, or even what it is. One is to witness the emergence – the emergency! – of images that have demanded to be made visible. The head: hood-shaped but flesh-coloured and, it appears, surgically sutured, so not a mask but a naked creature. The bottle: bloody red, lit by the light and watched by the head, so no mere still-life but the talisman of an alarmed scrutiny. The light: green like nature and shedding tiny grey bullet-rays, no neutral fixture but a funnel or megaphone or eye of intensity. The paint-handling is beautiful, with a beauty that in the comfortless context is heartbreaking. Think of it: to be so sensuously alert, so tender, so favoured, and yet to be subject to the damned head, the damned bottle, and the goddamned light! And what use is painting, which refuses – declines emphatically – to transcend any of this? But where would we be without painting, after all? Poor, smelly, indispensable painting.

The unraisably ponderous head of the *Painter in Bed* (plate 21) regards with single eye a shelf or smoke-vision of shoes – maybe all the shoes he has ever worn and worn out, all those intimate casualties of distance and soil. Painting equipment and some ambiguous other objects weigh upon or tumble off his chest, or does he have a chest? The bedcovers are an upright, striated slab of tremulous paint and line, an abstraction complete with mandalic red circle in the lower right corner and signed 'Philip Guston' (the famous painter) in the lower centre. What else? A dainty pink light and a bulbous red one dangle from above – the red one with a very pullable-looking pullchain, perhaps for use when one has had enough of this flayed, blood-suffused, liverish, irremediable apparition of things that don't add up. Again, given what it comes to, what a dirty trick it seems to have been made so marvellously sensitive! And still there is painting, for all the good it does: some slight, some provisional good.

Social and political themes have been adduced from Guston's use of hooded figures (Ku Klux Klan?) and heaps of legs (Holocaust?), and the connections are supported by his known left-liberalism. But this class of his imagery evokes a concern both more and less general than politics. One the one hand, it fits into a sort of swing-barrelled sense of emergency, a cosmic distress that can be exuded at full strength by anything at all – in *The Magnet* (plate 22), by a compass that seems to have started life as a clock, a fat light bulb, a painting of open water on a lumpish support, and a 'questionable' book. (The picture suggests a rebus communicating an urgent message, completely undecodable.) On the other hand, Guston's political nightmares have a strictly subjective, intimate particularity. Affected by the world but unable to affect it in return, the artist is stuck with his visions, which assume ambivalent roles in the tragicomedy of his inner life. A certain identification flows to the hooded spectres, and the vernacular rug in *Rug III* (plate 24) hints that mass murder, if that's what it is, has moved in and taken up domestic residence. In *Edge* (plate 25), the dismembered limbs are seen in a killing-ground ambience of red and black, but they are also made to form an insouciant, ghoulish chorus line.

The historic significance of Guston's late style has nothing directly to do with issues of abstraction versus figuration, still less with any 'return to the figure' (that unslayable journalistic chimera). The fundamental question Guston addressed was not how or what to paint, but *why:* the need for a reason sufficient to each painting and inescapably evident in each painting. Nothing less could recover conviction for an art gutted by the burn-out of modernist ideals. Guston did not reach for a solution, but surrendered to content near at hand, abolishing the priesthood of modern art by declaring that the painter is the same person when he is painting and when he is not painting. The same guilts, doubts, and obsessions afflict him inside the studio and out. Painting is one of his obsessions, one that he has privileged above the others but can no longer justify so privileging. Only by introducing it into the flow of his obsessions – incidentally foregrounding the continuum of his life and woes with the life and woes of a culture that has uses for painting – can he gain confidence in the activity as something seriously thinkable, leaving open the question of whether or not it is worth doing.

Only culture, over time, can decide whether an art has been worth doing. Culture has cast a vote for Guston, not simply by noting the resemblance of his late work to present fashions in painting but also by registering, however dimly, its radical truth. This is a truth about the artist as a victim of imagination. When all the heady theories, pretty stories, and other evasive circumlocutions about art are done, we come down to a lone, suffering consciousness in aroused communion with its own suffering. For instance, we come down to *Friend — To M.F.* (plate 26), Guston's great portrait of his close friend Morton Feldman, the composer (his big ear presumably for music). The similarity of this head to those in Guston's many self-portrayals suggests a kind of projected or symbiotic self-portrait. The head is turned away from the viewer – a rarity, to say the least, in portraiture. Nothing sinister seems implied by this disconcerting gesture. The massive head, heavily benign in its tobacco revery, is simply preoccupied, looking at or into something with bloodshot eye. That something is painting. The head regards the mysterious sky-blue field in which it is embedded: the painting field that is always full-face to painter and viewer alike. We are used to looking at this field. Guston here gives a demonstration of how to *watch* it: with reverent fear and helpless love.

Peter Schjeldahl   **Anselm Kiefer**

At the root of the scandals of this scandalous century is forgetfulness: on purpose, serving malign ideologies or naïve dreams of progress, and as a habit of carelessness, a hole in the head through which the world leaks away. Great modern artists have been great forgetters, for the most part. Modernism was a culture of forgetting, of euphorically or elegiacally saying goodbye. Anselm Kiefer is a great rememberer. Like no one else, he shows us that modernism is over – by remembering it. Kiefer forgets almost nothing, least of all things that many want most to forget. Retrieving inconvenient truths from the modern oubliette, he hangs them on a wall. He is our greatest artist not only for the matter of his work, its palimpsest of particular memories, but for its manner, which is the manner – the means, the protocol, the passion – of remembering.

Kiefer is a history painter, the first of consequence since Delacroix. His mode is public, rhetorical, even declamatory in a virtually pre-modern, early nineteenth-century way, and yet his sophisticated, ironic sensibility is exactly attuned to the post-modernist moment. By this seeming contradiction, Kiefer brackets – surrounds – the modern, considered as a zone of fissures and ruins. His great theme of German culture and its debacle in the Third Reich constitutes just a central fissure and ruined site, a master metaphor, of his vision. Its importance as an independent issue must not be denied, but Kiefer has been viciously misunderstood by those who have allowed it to blind them to the fullness of his art. For it is art as a civilising, redemptive force that is Kiefer's ultimate theme. In confronting the century's largest horror, he puts his hope and his ambition to the test. If, without evasion, art can deal with the Nazi catastrophe, he reasonably suggests, art can deal with anything.

Kiefer's work places unaccustomed demands on viewers. It is not enough simply to look at his pictures. One must *read* and take instruction from them. One must learn the historic and literary references, and if, like me, one has no German, it is necessary to seek translation of titles and texts. Such requirements have provoked lively resentment in some quarters; and certain other viewers, enthusiastic about Kiefer's visual splendours, have seemed to regard his allusions as pretentious nuisances, which thankfully can be ignored. But the critical element of Kiefer's greatness is not his aesthetic mastery, impressive as that is, but his interfolding of the aesthetic with other resources and capacities of the mind. His art is devised to assimilate and make available a maximum density of meaning: historical, poetic, and, in a fundamental sense, religious. Despite first appearances, little is hermetic or obscure in his enterprise. Properly informed, the viewer has ready access to the lyrical heights and cathartic depths of Kiefer's work, a *total* art-work which scorns the specialised pleasures of the museum to address humanity as a whole.

Kiefer's favoured motif is landscape: a ploughed or burned field with a high horizon, rendered in vertiginous perspective but smashed flat to the picture plane by an emphasis on materials and process. (The painterly topography is that of 'American', Abstract-Expressionist flatness and scale, given a 'French' spin of sensuous, nature-derived nuance: Kiefer forgets nothing of the modernist legacy.) The landscape often is a former battlefield which, to translate a Victor Hugo tag Kiefer has used, 'still quakes from the footsteps of fleeing giants': perhaps the forest where Hermann, in the first 'German victory', slaughtered Roman legions in AD9 or much-bloodied Mark Brandenburg County (which gave its name to the marching song 'Mark Heath, Mark Sand') or the site of this or that Wehrmacht operation in World War II. But there is no precise depiction – no landscape that could not be a peaceful, though perhaps burned-off rural field – because Kiefer's real landscape is of the mind, a sedimentary region of haunted and haunting memories and associations.

Memory is made heart-shattering by a child's lullaby in the early masterpiece *Maikäfer flieg* ('Cockchafer, Fly') (plate 27): What first appears to be a straggling line of soldiers or refugees on the horizon of a reeking field turns out to be a line of gently sorrowing words. 'Cockchafer, fly,' it reads. 'Father is in the war. Mother is in Pomerania. Pomerania is burned up.' *Bilderstreit* ('Iconoclastic Controversy') (plate 28) – a tank battle for a palette inscribed with names of eighth-century Byzantines who debated the permissibility of images – associates lethal power and intellectual terrorism. (More specific tanks roll in *Noch ist Polen nicht verloren IV* ('Poland Is Not Yet Lost') (plate 31). The stunning, huge woodcuts about Hermann's battle (plates 29 and 32), titled *Wege der Weltweisheit* ('Ways of Worldly Wisdom') convene generations of German politicians, creators, and thinkers who commented on that nationalistic symbol. (What would they make of it today?) The two paintings on blown-up photographs called *Wege: märkischer Sand* ('Ways: Mark Sand') respectively evoke, with place names, towns lost to Germany in the war (plate 33) and, with tongues of flame, a violent epiphany (plate 34). The magnificent *Ikarus=Märkischer Sand* ('Icarus=Mark Sand') (plate 36) implicates painting (a winged palette) in aspiration's archetypal calamity.

Kiefer's symbology of the artist, especially his use of the palette form, has been termed sentimental, and it used to strike me that way; but sentimentality is a failure of feeling, and Kiefer's purposeful clichés have gradually constellated a universe of feelings. Clichés are drained receptacles of truth. Kiefer puts truth, both old and new, back into them. In *Baum mit Palette* ('Tree with Palette') (plate 30), the tentacled leaden palette suggests art's source in a crude 'state of nature'. The *Palette am Seil* ('Palette on a Rope') (plate 35), with its flames, identifies art with both revelation and danger. Later, in pictures called *Dem unbekannten Maler* ('Monument to the Unknown Painter'), the palette would become the public talisman of a lost – a murdered – spiritual entity. Kiefer's palette is indefinitely changeable, an instrument for probing for meanings in the dark.

Kiefer's most courageous and desperately moving works are those inspired by two recurring lines in Paul Celan's great poem of the Holocaust, 'Death Fugue': 'your golden hair Margarete/your ashen hair Sulamith'. Margarete is Goethe's Margarete, symbol of Aryan womanhood. Sulamith, the loved one in the Song of Solomon, represents Jewish womanhood. This theme has appeared usually in landscape formats, with Margarete evoked by golden straw and Sulamith by ashy encrustations – adding an invocation of cyclical nature to Celan's elegy: As grasses sprout from the ground and are burned back into it, perhaps, the Holocaust was a harvest and is now a constituent of the German soil. A recent painting, the devastating *Sulamith* (plate 48), makes piercing use of one of the many motifs Kiefer has derived from Nazi architecture. In *Sulamith,* a mausoleum for German war heroes that was designed by Wilhelm Kreis is commandeered for a different rite: The torches on the walls, symbolic of the heroes, are blacked out, while on the distant altar burn the seven flames of the Biblical menorah.

To wrest creative energies from their terrible symbiosis with violence in German culture seems a task of Kiefer's works based on *Wölundlied* ('The Song of Wayland') (plates 43, 44, 45) and *Die Meistersinger* (plates 39, 42). The Edda tells the tale of Wayland, master blacksmith who, crippled by his king to keep him from straying, raped the king's daughter and killed his two sons (making drinking cups from their skulls), then forged wings for himself and flew away. Kiefer's visual association of this parable of evil with the 'scorched earth' of Germany sets up a troubling and profound reverberation. The Meistersinger is a symbol of the medieval flowering of Germanic culture at Nuremberg – the Nuremberg, later, of Hitler's rallies and of the war-crimes trials. Kiefer telescopes these meanings in paintings that may feature flares of colour, bright as clown motley, in collaged heaps of burned wood and straw. The effect is like an overlay of sounds: ancient song, Wagnerian anthem, screeching loudspeakers, the crash of war, the quiet telling of unbelievable horrors.

One of Kiefer's richest themes, advanced by him in a wide variety of forms and mediums, has been *Unternehmen Seelöwe* ('Operation Sea-lion'), of which plate 49 is a recent reworking. Operation Sea-lion was Hitler's plan to invade England. Having little experience of amphibious warfare, the German command rigged a French gymnasium with tubs of water and had officers play with model boats to reckon how the thing was done. This episode – a petty rehearsal for a titanic battle that never occurred – may fascinate Kiefer for its resemblance to artistic creation, which invests humble objects with cosmic significance. Employing, as he often has, toy warships and an old, vaguely coffin-shaped zinc bathtub he owns, Kiefer here plunks the tub in dramatic but innocent terrain under a dark sky. The faintly comical disjunction in scale between the ships and the tub, and between the tub and the landscape, enacts a dream-like reversal, by which monstrous forces of history are miniaturised and a modest rural locale is correspondingly giganticised. This brilliant image typifies Kiefer's humour, for which he has never received sufficient credit – perhaps because, as a species of Shakespearean lyrical irony, it is unalloyed with the nervous hysteria that demands release in laughter.

Kiefer's art holds out mighty rewards to all viewers who, having taken the trouble to learn his lexicon, can see with their own eyes, think with their own heads, and feel with their own hearts. Somehow, it should be possible to say this of all art, but really it isn't. Much of even great art – and modern art almost entirely – secretes as much as it reveals and exacts a ritual of initiation. In a realm of common histories and myths and, yes, clichés, Kiefer acts not to express or manipulate but purely to *empower* sensation, thought, and feeling. He provides grist to the mill that is every responsive and truly civilised human being. In so doing, he fans the fire of yearnings that spill far beyond art, becoming the vision of a world redeemed by wisdom and pity. It may be possible to overestimate Kiefer's importance to world culture in the late twentieth century, but at this point I don't quite see how.

Hilton Kramer **Malcolm Morley**

There is a wonderful passage in the text that Matisse wrote for *Jazz* in which he warns artists against the possibility of becoming prisoners of their own style and success. 'Un artiste', he wrote, 'ne doit jamais être prisonnier de lui-même, prisonnier d'une manière, prisonnier d'une réputation, prisonnier d'un succès . . . .' Often in my encounters with the paintings of Malcolm Morley in recent years I have thought of Matisse's observation, for Morley is an artist who seems to have taken this warning – or something like it – very much to heart and made it one of the bases of his creative work. As a result, his art may be seen to have developed as a succession of flights or turns from an acquired manner, and there are times when this sense of flight – and its corollary leap into something untried – appears to account for the unexpected course that is traced even in a single work. His is a volatile sensibility.

It was not to be expected, then, that a career so wedded to change and reversal would yield the artist a single or fixed reputation, and it hasn't. His first fame came with the photo-realist pop paintings he produced in the 1960s. His second fame, which today has brought him widespread recognition as one of the major painters of his time, dates from the later 1970s when he re-emerged as a more or less expressionist painter working in several distinct but related styles. If there is some underlying unity, aesthetic or spiritual, that joins the pop paintings of the 1960s with the expressionist paintings of more recent years in a perfect, unbroken continuum, this writer has failed to discover what it is. We are likely to be closer to a real understanding of the impulse at work in Morley's art if we abandon all thought of some underlying unity and focus instead on the different modes of vision that have governed his most distinctive efforts. In neither his art nor its development will we find a model of orderliness.

He was born in London in 1931, and spent much of the Second World War there. In his youth he went to sea, and also served a three-year prison term. It was in prison that he is said to have developed an interest in painting. His formal art training began at the Camberwell School of Arts and Crafts in 1952–3. He then studied at the Royal College of Art, completing his diploma in 1957. By that time he had already visited New York, having been prompted to do so by the exhibition called 'Modern Art in the United States', which The Museum of Modern Art sent to the Tate Gallery in 1956. In 1958 he moved to New York, where he continues to live and work today.

Although he had been drawn to New York by his interest in the abstract expressionists and worked for a time in an abstract mode after settling there, he made his solo exhibition debut in New York as a representational painter, showing landscape paintings at the Kornblee Gallery in 1964. Very soon thereafter he turned to a more pop-oriented style in the photo-realist paintings of ocean liners. Like much of pop art, the ocean liner paintings were based on commercial photographic images – in this case, colour post cards and travel advertisements – which were enlarged to a scale that made the finished pictures at once ironic and incongruous. Although the ocean liner pictures were painted with a studied, deadpan exquisiteness that was very stylish in the 1960s, this particular vein of cool, foppish irony was never Morley's forte, and he soon abandoned it in favour of something more robust. The emotional range of these pictures was clearly too narrow to accommodate the pressures that were building up in Morley to let loose with something freer and more compelling. What remains impressive in these paintings is their tonal purity, but in most other respects the photo-realist pictures remain enclosed in a kind of 'period' style – neat, clean, elegant, and somewhat lifeless – that called for the suspension of many of the painter's characteristic gifts.

It proved to be no easy matter, however, for Morley to move beyond this buttoned-up period style. When he did let loose, he did so with a good deal of violence and chaos. Attempting to appropriate the resources of expressionism as a means of endowing his art with a sort of raffish vitality, Morley nonetheless tried to remain loyal to the kind of pop iconography he had employed in the ocean liner pictures, and the results were anything but felicitous. Thus in the early 1970s he turned to Rauschenberg and Johns for inspiration, and to Jim Dine – the Dine of the early 1960s – for his model. This was an odd choice – representing, as it were, a step backward in time. The art which Morley now attempted to emulate consisted of combining objects – clothing, hardware, trinkets from the five and dime store, or anything else that came to hand – with unlovely, overloaded surfaces executed in a headlong parody of expressionist mannerisms. It was a model already moribund when Morley turned to it, quite as if he were determined to turn back the clock and go back to the early 1960s and start over, and there was no way even for a painter of his remarkable energy and drive to resuscitate this particular model with complete success.

Still – such are the paradoxes of artistic creation – this 'backward' move proved to have the desired catalytic effect for Morley's work. Starting over was pretty much what he was attempting to do in these failed paintings of the early 1970s. The truth is, though they *are* failed pictures (and thus raise legitimate questions about the place to be assigned to them in his œuvre as a whole), they *did* represent a new start for the artist, giving him for the first time a purchase on the kind of expressionist fluency that he subsequently developed into some of the most powerful pictures of the late 1970s and early 1980s – paintings that have made Morley one of the stellar figures of the neo-expressionist movement and thus a new model for other artists. To accomplish this change, however, he had to perform some fairly radical surgery on the 1960s model he was working from. All those unlovely objects had to be stripped away from the picture surface – the coil of rope and plastic bag and women's shoes attached to *Piccadilly Circus* (1973), for example, and the straw hat and plastic rose attached to *Untitled Souvenirs, Europe* (1973) (plate 55) – and something akin to a more traditional painterly syntax re-established as a governing principle.

He was no doubt aided in this effort by the plunge he made into paraphrasing and parodying the old (and some not so old) masters in the late 1960s and early 1970s. The paintings that Morley produced in this line, from *Vermeer, Portrait of the Artist in his Studio* (1968) (plate 51) to *Picasso Bridge* (1972) (plate 53) and *School of Athens* (1972) (plate 54), have a multiple interest for us. They are certainly to be seen as tokens of the artist's ambition. They are also deliberate, self-conscious acts of aesthetic appropriation. That they contain passages of painterly eloquence

19

that far exceed anything Morley had achieved earlier on in his work is both interesting in itself and important as an augury of things still to come in his work. That they are uneven in quality and inconsistent in conception is also a sign of that tendency we have already noted toward unexpected reversals and sudden turns.

To attempt a great deal, to subvert an idea even in the course of perfecting it, to aspire to many and sometimes contradictory things at once – this, it seems to me, is the very essence of the dynamism that governs Morley's painting and gives it its special quality. His gifts are never in question, it seems to me, though what he does with them may sometimes be. At his best he is simply a marvellous painter – and a painter of the marvellous. That he is also a quirky and unsteady painter, given to flights of inspired fancy – a kind of imaginative mania – that often exceeds his powers of control, is also true. There is a deep neurotic strain in his work, but there is also a kind of classical yearning in it as well. He is an artist of divided, indeed warring, sensibilities. If this accounts for the highly dramatic aura that attaches itself to much of his recent work – and I believe it does – it may also explain something about its waywardness and wilfulness. In Morley there is clearly a conflict between the cool, classical artist he sometimes yearns to be and the hot, romantic fantasist he more often feels compelled to be.

The paradox of all this is easily traced in his paintings of the 1980s – by far the most powerful paintings he has yet produced. While some of the finest of them – *La Plage* and *Landscape with Horses* (both 1980), *Landscape with Bullocks* (1981), and *Macaws, Bengals, with Mullet* (1982) (plate 62) – owe much of their quality to the role which a more traditional ('classical') syntax is allowed to play in their realisation, the artist himself is so far from being at ease with it that he takes considerable pains to disrupt and subvert it in some of his most ambitious efforts. I have in mind such pictures as *Camels and Goats* (1980) (plate 59), *Arizonac* (1981) (plate 60), *The Palms of Vai* (1982) and *Farewell to Crete* (1984) (plate 63). Is it yet another paradox of Morley's work that his most ambitious paintings – and there is none more ambitious than *Farewell to Crete* – are not always the most coherent or integrated, that they make a point of being unresolved and open to further exploration?

Be that as it may, since his turn toward the expressionist mode over a decade ago Morley seems to have adopted a deliberate policy of producing at least two very distinct types of work – pictures that, on the one hand, are carefully integrated in design and fairly placid, even pastoral, in their imagery *(Indian Winter,* 1981 (plate 61), for example), and, on the other, pictures that are highly disjunctive both in their imagery and their syntax. The latter, apparently, are an attempt to achieve by purely painterly means the kind of violent shifts and symbolic juxtapositions once accomplished by the introduction of incongruous physical objects à la Jim Dine. For this purpose Morley now draws upon a vein of archaic and primitivistic iconography that is blatantly contrasted with the purely naturalistic elements in painting. The aspiration, I suppose, is to create an art that addresses the spectator at two levels simultaneously, the mythic/symbolic and the naturalistic. This is precisely the kind of aspiration that inspired some of the greatest paintings of the expressionist tradition – among others, the magnificent series of triptychs that were Max Beckmann's crowning achievement. (We find its literary counterpart in *The Waste Land* and a good many other modernist poems.) It is, in fact, one of the classic aspirations of high modernism, and one from which painters turned away when they lost their faith in the aesthetic efficacy of a 'literary' subject matter (as it is usually called). It tells us much about Morley's vision – as well as his ambition – that he should aspire to produce an art at this level of complexity and completeness.

Whatever the degree of success these paintings achieve and however much they remain haunted by their lack of some final integrating vision, what they nonetheless boast an abundance of is a kind of heated feeling and visceral intensity that we hardly expected to find in pictorial art in the days when it was so completely dominated by the ideals of clarity, irony, and orderly form. Morley has come a long way since those neat ocean liner paintings of the 1960s. And if he has so far shown a greater mastery over and confidence in the naturalistic component of the style he now aspires to, he has nonetheless succeeded in the use he has made of its mythical and fantastic elements in reviving the possibility of something far grander. At this stage of his development Morley is clearly an artist still reaching for something he has not yet fully achieved, however close he seems at times to getting there and however much we are engaged and moved by the spectacle of his unremitting assault on his objective. Both the aspiration itself and what he has achieved in attempting to realise it, however, have decisively changed the art of our time.

Rudi Fuchs   **Sigmar Polke**

The panting crocodile with the sad eyes reaches out into the hell of black for the drifting bottle. The sea is leaning on its notched back. Oh, these old European pictures! From the open mouth, long flames of red fire are spouting forth, curving upward along the black and ending in a blue and yellow flowery star. Down along the fiery tongue slides the purple monkey, hitting the crocodile's nose with a little blue cross. The monkey wears a red and yellow hat, with a feather, like somebody on holiday. He clings to one of the legs of the acutely myopic Koala bear, reminiscent of Australia but not unlike our old friend Mickey Mouse either. The Koala, in the meantime, balances with his other leg on the head of the red-hatted monkey (who is hitting the crocodile) and leans against a yellow and blue garland, cascading down towards the sea, ending in a branch with flowers. An opening in the cascade provides us with a glimpse of a pleasant lake upon which three creatures of unknown origin are paddling in a canoe. To the south of the garland we see the bright, yellow sky against which the erect penis stands out like a lighthouse. In the meantime, my friend, a greenish snow has started to fall on the otherwise sunny scene. Other monkeys are enjoying themselves. One, in blueish purple, is climbing up a thin line rising from the flowery star at the end of the crocodile's tongue of fire. He is pushed by a curving, brown arrow. It is a funny little monkey – with its little wings it looks like a fairy-tale insect, but with its blue horns it looks like a frightened devil, though more out of Gustave Doré than Hieronymus Bosch. What the chequered pattern and the number three are doing up there I don't know. The other monkey is hanging from a branch, as monkeys do, hanging aloft or pulling forward over the blue like the unlikely cyclist, part Red Indian and part smiling Byzantine Madonna. In the upper left-hand corner of the painting the horizon, like a comet, is shooting past.

Obviously this painting (*Affen* (plate 74)) could be described in a different way. But in whichever way one wants to read it, the conclusion is always the same: that the painting, like virtually all of Polke's paintings, is a conglomerate of images or a sequence of images in balanced *montage*. In *Affen* (which may not be a key-picture but which is typical of Polke's 'associative' method), the images follow one another in a linear pattern, like a meander, producing one another, as curling smoke produces *figurettes* – a chain of motifs as in a fairy-tale. In other, maybe more familiar pictures the images are overlayed, a telescopic sequence in depth, in which the images float, intermingle and penetrate one another. The 'layers' become ambiguous. In paintings such as *Bunnies* and *Rasterbild mit Palmen* (plates 66, 67), or other pictures from that period using the 'screening' technique, the image is blurred: the technique becomes a pattern which conceals and reveals at the same time, leaving the eye to guess. Even relatively straightforward and ironic paintings such as *Liebespaar II* (plate 65) carry with them, in their slipstream, a series of other images. *Liebespaar II* is not an image to *exclude* other images. That is what a classic, pre-modern painting does: Rubens's matrimonial portrait of himself and Isabella Brant for instance, known to art historians as *Die Gartenlaube,* wants you to forget other images or wants to replace other images. In *Liebespaar II,* however, the image is one which reviews a wide range of other images; one in particular came floating to the surface to determine the painting's look, but other images, similar in sentiment, are implied.

This method of constructing images, often from completely different sources and which flow into one another, occurs also in other areas of Polke's artistic activity – notably in his films and photographic work. It is important to point this out as all the different aspects of this extraordinarily rich and complex *œuvre* finally come together in what seems to be the central concern in Polke's art: the task of how to generate an image, how to find it and how to articulate it. A central stylistic consensus which regulates the conception and formulation of images doesn't exist in our culture (unlike the age of Baroque). The individual artist has to invent and manipulate his own rules. In most cases a certain type of regulation is used: formal conditions a picture must fulfill. The clearest expression of this approach is found in the work of artists like Sol LeWitt which, in order to be so, had also to be abstract. Polke wasn't prepared to accept abstraction because it would take away enormous iconographic possibilities. This then leads to a picture structure in which an image is not imposed but in which the image detaches itself from another image (leaving the previous image intact). A stain of paint may become the shadow of another form, the line in one image may become the outline of something else. In his studio, which in itself is a great and labyrinthine storehouse of images found and collected for further use (taken from books, magazines, newspapers), I have seen a progressive series of Xerox-copies (each one copying the previous one) in which astounding transformations have taken place: the original image, culled from some magazine, changed beyond recognition, has become another image. The Xerox-series I saw wasn't produced with a particular goal in mind; it was simply waiting to be used. There was something allegorical about it: it signified the way in which the artist's mind should work, pushing beyond the cultural limits of imagination – going over the top of a mountain and discovering an unknown land.

In the early Renaissance, central perspective was not invented for aesthetic reasons. Equally, Sigmar Polke's search for an extremely complex and visually manageable picture, a picture without spatial direction, is not meant to be just an *aesthetic* contribution to art. For him, a painting is as much a *passage* in his 'research programme' as is film or photography. Although his work has often been compared to American Pop Art, it bears little or no relationship, since he is not searching for the emblematic image. What he is seeking is an imagery complex enough to deal with the extraordinarily complex nature of our visual surroundings – which have changed our perception. Life in a modern city, amid a bombardment of visual information, calls for a quite different vision from that of the inhabitant of the city of the Middle Ages. Hence modern pictures must be different. Polke needs refined pictorial means to help in his quest. His experiments with the properties of paint, chemicals and unusual pigments, have in themselves no meaning. He is not looking for more beautiful colours but is attempting to expand the range of possibilities and techniques in his *repertoire.* Adding certain chemicals or acids to certain types of lacquer is, for Polke, exactly the same operation as combining two absolutely disparate images – letting the one enter into the other to see what happens.

Polke's pictorial discourse, his artistic conviction, is of a philosophical and political nature; to push that conviction into the world, to articulate it, he needs a certain type of painting which then, to be viable, has to be superior painting. The world in 1984 no longer concentrates on a few great images; and if it does, in Polke's view, it shouldn't. Whatever control is exercised over the image, by politicians, priests or advertisers, should be broken down. Visual democracy is the floating image, many floating images, cutting through one's line of vision, images blurring other images, a world of images without any visual hierarchy. Thus in Polke's iconographies one finds the sublime next to the ridiculous. None of his pictures has a precise centre, beginning or end, nor a recognisable style. Where do you focus in the Hannibal painting (plate 79), what do you see and what does it mean? His imagery is there to unsettle you, to take away your hope that the world changes only slowly and measurably. It changes as it changes and painting has to keep pace with it. That, precisely, is Polke.

Hilton Kramer   **Julian Schnabel**

It has been the peculiar fate of Julian Schnabel to become, and at a very early age too, the most controversial painter of his generation. He has also been one of the most successful. Well before he was thirty – he was born in 1951 – his work was the subject of heated critical discussion. Because it was in such demand by collectors and museums, moreover, it quickly became the subject of the kind of rumour and gossip that shifts attention from the art to the artist and his career, his income, his dealer, and his personal life. All of which, in turn, prompted the artist himself to make statements and grant interviews that – more often than not – contributed more to the haze of publicity surrounding his work than to its clarification or understanding. Thus, from the very beginning of his public career, Schnabel has been the very archetype of the young artist plying his wares in the limelight – which, though it guarantees a certain kind of visibility, is rarely the best light in which to view an artist's work dispassionately or judiciously.

On the other hand, there is no denying that there is something appropriate about the clamour that has greeted Schnabel's work, for his is both a clamorous and a 'public' style. However subjective and allusive his imagery may be at times, the work that contains it is always conceived on a scale and in a manner which preclude an intimate or merely 'private' response. It deliberately sets out to overwhelm the spectator with a greater multiplicity of impressions than can be easily assimilated in a single viewing, and to so orchestrate those impressions that a certain conflict in interpreting the result is, as it were, built into the very experience of seeing the work. An element of bluster, of sheer assault on our senses, on our expectations, and on our taste, is never entirely absent from the artist's calculations. Often, in fact, it is the dominant note that is struck in picture after picture, so that we come to feel that it is this element, more than any other, that supplies Schnabel's work with its principal momentum.

It was inevitable, perhaps, that this element of bluster would be deplored when Schnabel's work first came to light, and that it would remain a controversial issue even after the artist had become an established figure on the international art scene. For no other aspect of his work so vividly signifies the change in artistic outlook that Schnabel's pictures have been taken to represent, and it is the implications of this change, quite as much as the artist's own exploitation of them, that lie at the heart of the controversy which has enveloped his art from the outset. To grasp what this change in outlook has entailed is therefore essential to any fundamental understanding of what Schnabel has achieved – or, for that matter, has failed to achieve – in his work.

Schnabel belongs to an artistic generation that was born into an art world ready and eager to receive an assault on its established norms. It was not an art world that could be said to be characterised by the old conflict between an avant-garde and a benighted, complacent public, firm in its resistance to new ideas. That particular conflict had been amicably resolved in the 1960s, and in the new art world which came into existence in the aftermath of that resolution, a premium was placed on precisely the kind of audacity and innovation that public opinion had formerly made it a point of rejecting. At the same time, however, an implicit limit was placed on what the permissible parameters of audacity and innovation might be. What seemed to be excluded from this otherwise open invitation to innovation was anything that smacked of backsliding, anything that suggested a reversion to or revival of artistic practices which had already been rejected in the name of innovation itself.

What, then, most distinguished this new art world at the moment when Schnabel and the artists of his generation were preparing to make their entry into it was the persistence of an orthodoxy – a specifically modernist orthodoxy – which presented itself, somewhat misleadingly, as an open situation. There was much about the artistic situation that *was* open, to be sure, but there was much that remained closed, too. What defined the new orthodoxy, above all, was the aesthetic of minimalism, which had emerged as the principal heir to the modernist tradition, and the various challenges to the authority of minimalism to be found among the post-minimalist abstract styles of the 1970s. Within this tidy, 'open' dialogue of abstract styles ample provision was made for the re-introduction of expressionist gesture as well as for an art more overtly decorative than minimal art had been concerned to be. But the dialogue itself nonetheless contained an important prohibition, and what was prohibited was precisely the introduction of the kind of expressionist imagery likely to pose a threat to abstraction itself.

It was just there, however, in that realm of expressionist imagery so long despised and rejected by the exponents of modernist orthodoxy, that an opportunity presented itself to Schnabel and others of his emerging generation to alter the course of art in their time, and the opportunity was seized with a display of energy and ambition, and a lack of inhibition and decorum, that has left heads reeling and tongues wagging ever since. Nothing quite like this rupture in taste, in aesthetic orientation, and in the sheer look of painting had occurred since the advent of pop art nearly twenty years earlier, and whereas pop art had shocked its initial public with a show of campy humour and facetious charm – by being, in effect, almost too easy and accessible to be taken seriously – the new expressionism looked to be in dead earnest. Suddenly painting had become grave, mysterious, and messy again, and not in any of the familiar ways. It had also become boisterous, swaggering, and 'tough'. Charm, elegance, and reductive understatement were all firmly rejected, and so was the tendency to anorexic aestheticism that had come to characterise the minimalist impulse at its outermost extremes. Excess and surfeit were embraced as a principle of vitality.

In the case of Schnabel, who straightaway established himself in the forefront of this development, the tendency to excess and surfeit was concentrated as much on the handling of the picture surface as it was on the creation of a new imagery. The priority that Schnabel gave to building up the surfaces of outsize pictures with plaster, broken crockery, and sundry other materials and objects was by no means an entirely original idea, of course. There was ample precedent for it in the work of Rauschenberg and Johns. Yet the spirit informing this familiar practice was significantly altered. All trace of Duchampian elegance and supercilious irony was gone, and in its place was the expressionist bluster and bombast that was to give Schnabel's work its own special resonance. The expressionist mode is, by its very nature, inhospitable to dandyish elegance and neo-dada irony. Its forte lies in its unsparing forthrightness, and this was the quality that Schnabel made palpable in the very density and materiality of the surfaces he employed.

As a corollary to the physical properties with which Schnabel endowed these surfaces he was equally forthright in the conspicuous use he made of overscale images appropriated from literature, films, photographs, religious symbols, and other paintings – images that blatantly proclaimed their presence without readily disclosing their meaning. With the energy of a madcap anthologist scooping up the fragments and tag ends of anything that interested him in the abandoned debris of contemporary cultural life, Schnabel seemed to be as much in search of the meaning that these images might have for him – and for us – as he was in search of the images themselves. His principle in selecting them appeared to be random and associational, and it was certainly anything but systematic. Yet a rough consistency could nonetheless be discerned in the pattern they traced from picture to picture, for these images tended to be drawn from the world of culture rather than from the realm of nature. They tended, too, to have an archetypal rather than a discrete character, and to be used less as subjects than as symbols. However incongruous their juxtaposition might be in a given picture, Schnabel's images were also consistent in evoking something akin to an elegiac attitude toward their content. There has indeed always been something ghostlike in the appearance of these images in Schnabel's pictures – something that suggests that the images do not so much occupy these pictures as haunt them. As vivid as the images are to the eye, they tend to hover on the picture surface without quite taking root in its material existence, almost as if they were images flashed on a screen. Whereas the surfaces in Schnabel's pictures have been invariably dense, sensuous, and palpable in the extreme, his images have generally given the impression of something conjured. We are never quite certain about what to make of them. We are never quite certain that Schnabel has known what to make of them.

What this suggests is that there is a certain disjunction in Schnabel's work between surface and image – between the work's material realisation, on the one hand, and its imaginative conception, on the other. Among the new expressionists of Schnabel's generation, he is by no means alone in this respect. To one degree or another, a similar disjunction will be found to characterise a good deal of the work of his contemporaries as well. If it tends to be more conspicuous in Schnabel than elsewhere, it is only because everything in his work has a tendency to be highly charged and bluntly stated – he is an artist who shuns the lower registers of expression in favour of saturation and a revved up intensity. That is one of the things that gives him a natural affinity for the expressionist mode.

The very nature of this disjunction between surface and image tells us something important, I believe, about the fate of the expressionist impulse in Schnabel's generation. It reminds us of how profoundly a work of art remains tethered to its moment in cultural history – to the whole complex of beliefs, assumptions, and received ideas that comes to dominate the conception of art at a given point in time – even when the artist himself is in open rebellion against the artistic status quo. In Schnabel's case, we are reminded of the extent to which his art remains tethered to the triumph of minimalism and the various aesthetic strategies which the artists of the 1970s adopted in their resistance to it. To the art that belongs to this anti-minimalist resistance the critic Robert Pincus-Witten has given the name 'maximalism', and it is a term that describes Schnabel (among others) very well. For it offers us a useful clue as to why the surface in Schnabel's work, whether he is painting on velvet or a dropcloth or working in high relief with plaster, crockery, and other materials, tends to achieve a more persuasive authority than the images that trace a ghostlike course upon that surface. It suggests that the crux of the anti-minimalist resistance was to be found precisely in this question of surfaces and their visual attributes, and that the problem of imagery was, perforce, a matter of secondary importance.

It is in the nature of minimal art to give an absolute priority to surface and scale, and to render all other considerations subsidiary if not actually nugatory. In minimal art, surface and form are coextensive; so are surface and expression. The integrity of surface must therefore be regarded as absolute and inviolate. It follows, then, that any attempt to resist or transcend the strictures of the minimalist aesthetic is likely to make the violation of that surface its first and most fundamental interest. And it is in this act of artistic violation, by whatever means it takes, that the crucial breach with minimalism occurs. Once this violation of surface has been achieved, the question of introducing images into the artistic equation is a matter of discretion – which is to say, a secondary consideration. It is not the introduction of images – and still less is it the specific indentity of those images – that has defined the fundamental break. In the anti-minimalist art that Pincus-Witten dubbed 'maximalist', it scarcely matters whether images are employed or not. It is from the urge to alter the surface – to open it up to a greater multiplicity of visual sensation than minimal art allows – that the new aesthetic impulse derives its momentum.

This is one reason – the main reason, I believe – why Schnabel's radical modification of the placid minimalist surface in painting has proved to be more persuasive than his use of images. The minimalist aesthetic, with its strict prohibitions, provided him with a well-defined *donnée* he could act upon and transform with all the expressionist bluster that was natural to his sensibility. It gave him, so to speak, a tradition that could be overturned, and overturn it he did. But there was no comparable tradition to act upon and transform in the realm of pictorial image-making. There he was on his own – a free-lance, as it were, obliged to create an iconography out of his own imagination and out of his own cultural situation, and with no certainty that the images he introduced into his work would have the resonance and meaning for others that they appeared to have for him. His response to this challenge has been to adopt the outlook of a scavenger anthologist for whom the sheer multiplicity of images is inevitably more important than the identity of any single one of them. This has yielded him some striking results at times, yet the question of exactly which images are necessary to his art and which are merely an added-on component of it remains unresolved. And this, in turn, suggests that the revitalisation of the expressionist aesthetic which lies at the heart of his work also remains to be completed.

Plates

Dimensions are given first in inches, then in
centimetres.
Height precedes width precedes depth, unless
otherwise indicated.

GEORG BASELITZ

1
Partisan
1965
Oil on canvas
64 ×52 (162 ×132)

GEORG BASELITZ

2
MMM in G und A
1961/62/66
Oil on canvas
78×58 (195×145)

GEORG BASELITZ

3
Kullervos Füsse
1967
Oil on canvas
64×51 (162×130)

GEORG BASELITZ

4 (following page)
B. für Larry
1967
Oil on canvas
98½×79 (250×200)

5 (following page)
Zwei Meissener Waldarbeiter
1967
Oil on canvas
98½×79 (250×200)

4

GEORG BASELITZ

6
Graue Hunde, Drei Streifen
1967/68
Oil on canvas
64×51 (162×130)

7 (opposite)
Waldarbeiter
1968/69
Oil on canvas
98½×79 (250×200)

GEORG BASELITZ

8 (following page)
Waldarbeiter
1968
Oil on canvas
98½×79 (250×200)

9 (following page)
Dreieck zwischen Arm und Rumpf
1977
Oil on canvas
98½×79 (250×200)

8

9

GEORG BASELITZ

10
Akt und Flasche (diptych)
1977
Oil and tempera on wood
2 panels, Each: 98½×67 (250×170)

GEORG BASELITZ

11
Portrait und Adler (diptych)
1978
Oil and tempera on wood
2 panels, Each: 98½×67 (250×170)

GEORG BASELITZ

12
Die Frau in der Tür
1978
Oil and tempera on canvas
130×98½ (330×250)

GEORG BASELITZ

13
Night in Tunisia II
1980
Oil on canvas
98½×79 (250×200)

GEORG BASELITZ

14
Die Mädchen von Olmo
1981
Oil on canvas
98½ × 94½ (250 × 248)

GEORG BASELITZ

15
Weg vom Fenster
1982
Oil on canvas
98 1/2 × 98 1/2 (250 × 250)

GEORG BASELITZ

16
Der Trommler
1982
Oil on canvas
98½ × 130 (250×330)

GEORG BASELITZ

17
Untitled
1982
Painted wood
98½×36×24 (250×90×60)

GEORG BASELITZ

18
Die Dornenkrönung
1983
Oil on canvas
117×97½ (297·2×247·7)

GEORG BASELITZ

19
Nachtessen in Dresden
1983
Oil on canvas
110×177 (280×450)

PHILIP GUSTON

20
Head, Bottle, Light
1969
Oil on canvas
20 ×22 (50·8 ×55·9)

PHILIP GUSTON

21
Painter in Bed
1973
Oil on canvas
60 ×104 (152·4 ×264·2)

PHILIP GUSTON

22
The Magnet
1975
Oil on canvas
67½×80½ (171·5×204·5)

PHILIP GUSTON

23
Frame
1976
Oil on canvas
74 ×116 (188 ×294·6)

PHILIP GUSTON

24
Rug III
1976
Oil on canvas
69×110½ (175·3×280·7)

PHILIP GUSTON

25
Edge
1976
Oil on canvas
80×124¾ (203·3×316·9)

PHILIP GUSTON

26
Friend – to M.F.
1978
Oil on canvas
68 × 88 (172·7 × 223·5)

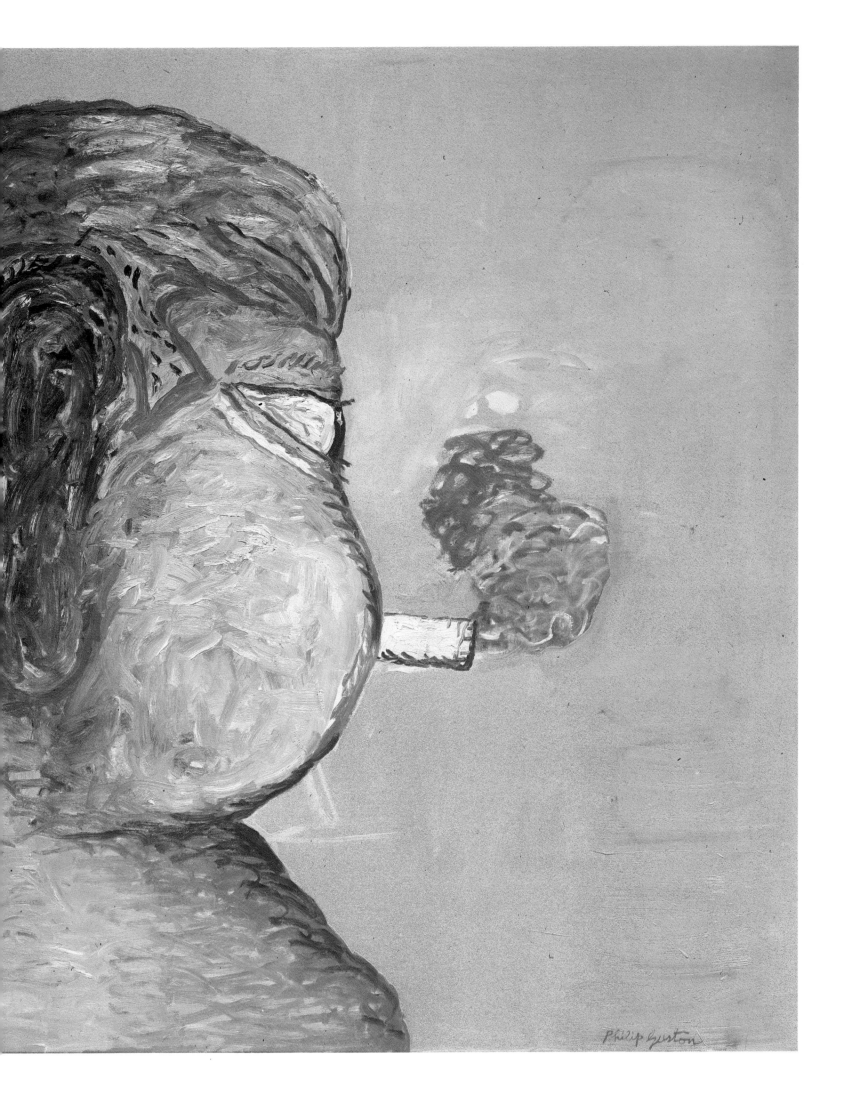

ANSELM KIEFER

27
Maikäfer flieg
1974
Oil on burlap
86⅝×118 (220×300)

28
Bilderstreit
1976/77
Oil on canvas
128×130 (325×330)

ANSELM KIEFER

29
Wege der Weltweisheit: die Hermannsschlacht
1978
Woodcut in 31 parts on blotting and handmade
paper, acrylic and shellac
133⁷/₈ × 137³/₄ (340 × 350)

ANSELM KIEFER

30
Baum mit Palette
1978
Oil on canvas with lead object
114¼×73 (290×185)

Baum mit Palette
1978
Oil on canvas with lead object
114¼×73 (290×185)

ANSELM KIEFER

31
Noch ist Polen nicht verloren IV
1978
Oil on canvas
75×112 (190×285)

ANSELM KIEFER

32
Wege der Weltweisheit: die Hermannsschlacht
1978
Woodcut in several parts on blotting and handmade
paper, emulsion, acrylic, and shellac on canvas
114¼×78¾ (290×200)

ANSELM KIEFER

33
Wege: märkischer Sand
1980
Oil, emulsion, shellac, sand, photograph (on
projection paper) on canvas
110×150 (280×380)

ANSELM KIEFER

34
Wege: märkischer Sand
1980
Acrylic, sand, photograph (on projection paper) on
burlap
100½×141¾ (255×360)

ANSELM KIEFER

35
Palette am Seil
1981
Oil and acrylic on canvas
82⁵/₈×128 (210×320)

ANSELM KIEFER

36
Ikarus=Märkischer Sand
1981
Oil, emulsion, shellac, sand, photograph (on
projection paper) on canvas
114¹/₄× 141³/₄ (290×360)

ANSELM KIEFER

37
Dein blondes Haar, Margarete (diptych)
1981
Oil and straw on canvas
Each panel: 46½ ×86 (118 ×218)
Overall: 46½ ×177 (118 ×449·6)

ANSELM KIEFER

38
Die drei Nornen (Urd Werdandi Skuld)
1981
Oil on canvas
66×75 (168×190)

ANSELM KIEFER

39
Die Meistersinger
1981
Oil, acrylic, straw on canvas
73 × 130 (185 × 330)

ANSELM KIEFER

40
Margarethe
1981
Oil and straw on canvas
110 × 150 (280 × 380)

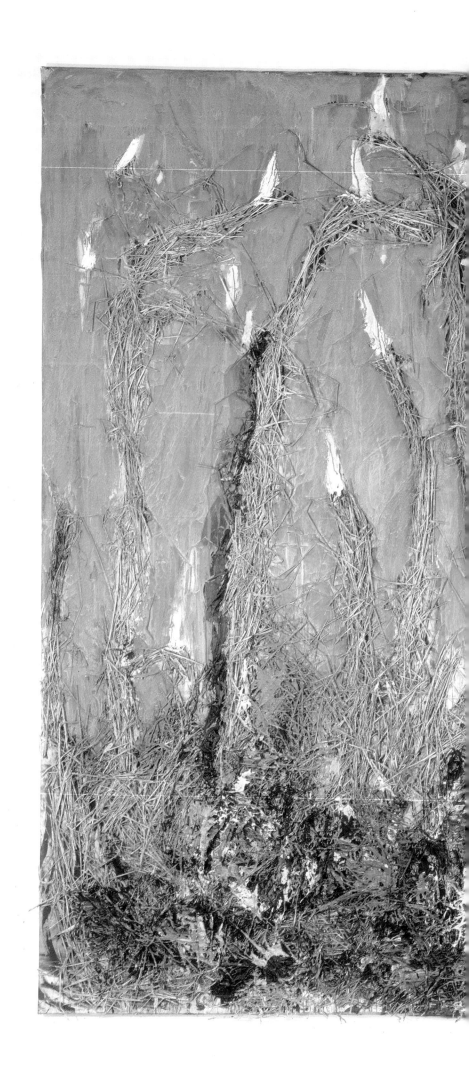

ANSELM KIEFER

41
Gilgamesch im Zedernwald
1981/82
Oil and straw on canvas
78³/₄ × 114¹/₄ (200 × 290)

ANSELM KIEFER

42
Die Meistersinger
1982
Oil, acrylic, straw and cardboard on canvas
110×150 (280×380)

ANSELM KIEFER

43
Wölundlied
1982
Oil, emulsion, straw, photograph (on projection
paper) on canvas with lead wing
110×150 (280×380)

ANSELM KIEFER

44
Wölundlied
1982
Oil, emulsion, straw, photograph (on projection
paper) on canvas with lead wing
110×150 (280×380)

ANSELM KIEFER

45
Wölundlied
1982
Oil, emulsion, straw, photograph (on projection
paper) on canvas with iron, wood and metal tongs
110×150 (280×380)

ANSELM KIEFER

46
Der Rhein
1982
Woodcut in several parts on blotting and handmade
paper, mounted on canvas
118×150 (300×380)

ANSELM KIEFER

47
Heliogabal
1983
Oil, emulsion, woodcut, shellac, acrylic,
and straw on canvas
110×110 (280×280)

ANSELM KIEFER

48
Sulamith
1983
Oil, emulsion, woodcut, shellac, acrylic, and straw
on canvas
114¼×145¾ (290×370)

ANSELM KIEFER

49
Unternehmen Seelöwe
1983/84
Oil, emulsion, shellac, acrylic, straw, photograph (on projection paper) on canvas
150×218½ (380×555)

MALCOLM MORLEY

50
SS Amsterdam in front of Rotterdam
1966
Acrylic on canvas
62×84 (157·5×213·5)

MALCOLM MORLEY

51
Vermeer, Portrait of the Artist in his Studio
1968
Acrylic on canvas
105×87 (266·5×221)

MALCOLM MORLEY

52
Safety is Your Business
1971
Oil on canvas
88 × 110 (224 × 280)

MALCOLM MORLEY

53
Picasso Bridge
1972
Oil on canvas
48 ×66 (122 ×168)

MALCOLM MORLEY

54
School of Athens
1972
Oil and acrylic on canvas
67 × 94 ½ (170 × 240)

MALCOLM MORLEY

55 (following page)
Untitled Souvenirs, Europe
1973
Oil and mixed media on canvas with objects
attached
96¼ × 68¼ (244·5 × 173·3)

56 (following page)
SS France
1974
Oil and mixed media on canvas with objects
attached
72 × 64 (183 × 162·5)

57
Age of Catastrophe
1976
Oil on canvas
60×96 (152·5×244)

MALCOLM MORLEY

58
Out Dark Spot
1978
Oil on canvas
72⅝×98¾ (185·3×250·8)

MALCOLM MORLEY

59
Camels and Goats
1980
Oil on canvas
66½×100 (169×254)

MALCOLM MORLEY

60
Arizonac
1981
Oil on canvas
80×105 (203×266·5)

MALCOLM MORLEY

61
Indian Winter
1981
Oil on canvas
53×77 (134·6×195·6)

MALCOLM MORLEY

62
Macaws, Bengals, with Mullet
1982
Oil on canvas
120×80 (305×203)

MALCOLM MORLEY

61
Indian Winter
1981
Oil on canvas
53×77 (134·6×195·6)

MALCOLM MORLEY

62
Macaws, Bengals, with Mullet
1982
Oil on canvas
120×80 (305×203)

MALCOLM MORLEY

63
Farewell to Crete
1984
Oil on canvas
80×164 (203·2×416·6)

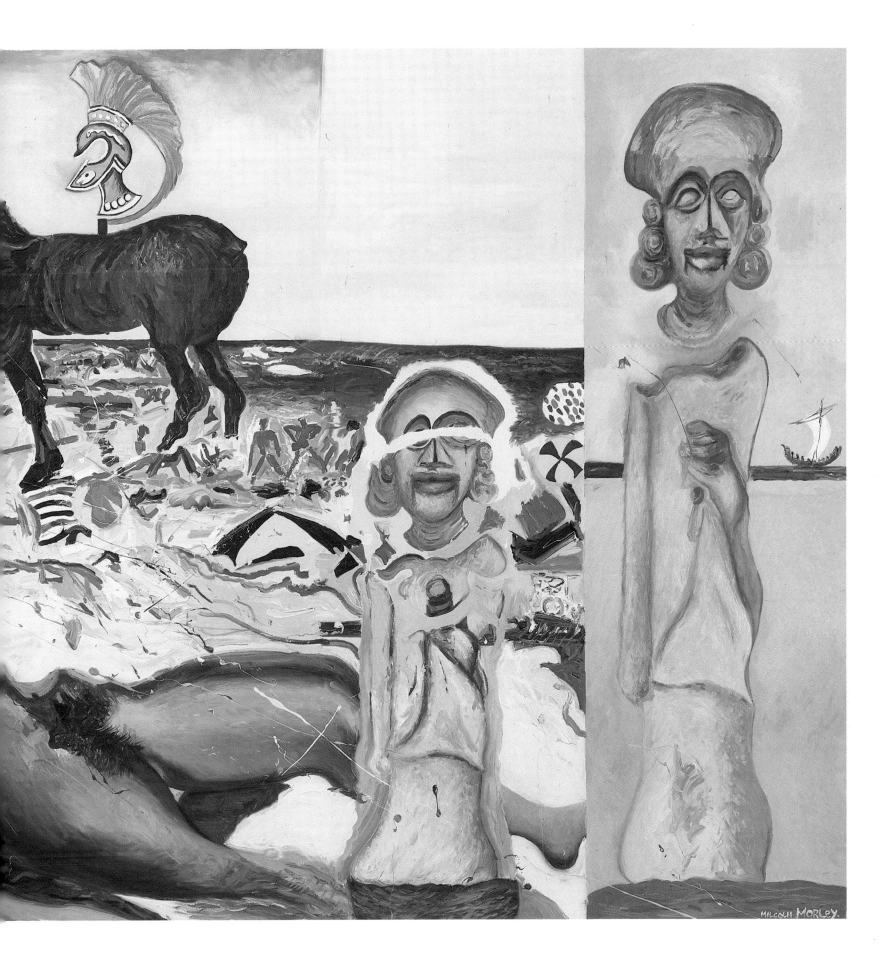

SIGMAR POLKE

64
Plastik-Wannen
1964
Oil on canvas
37 × 47¼ (94 × 120)

SIGMAR POLKE

65
Liebespaar II
1965
Oil and enamel on canvas
75 × 55 (190 × 140)

SIGMAR POLKE

66
Bunnies
1966
Oil on canvas
59×39½ (150×100)

SIGMAR POLKE

67
Rasterbild mit Palmen
1966
Oil on canvas
52×44 (130×110)

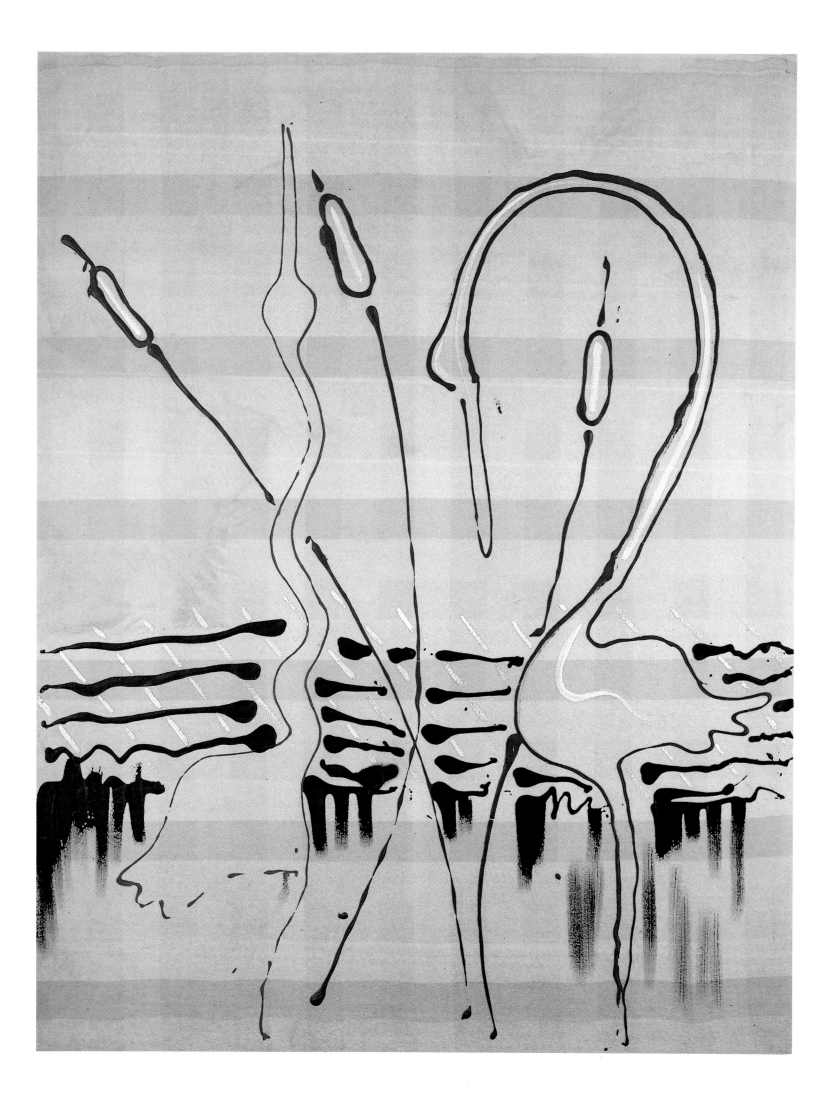

SIGMAR POLKE

68
Reiherbild II
1968
Dispersion on flannel
74³/₄ × 59 (190 × 150)

SIGMAR POLKE

69
Wolldeckenbild mit kleinen weissen Quadraten
1968
Dispersion on wool blanket
59 × 49¹/₄ (150 × 125)

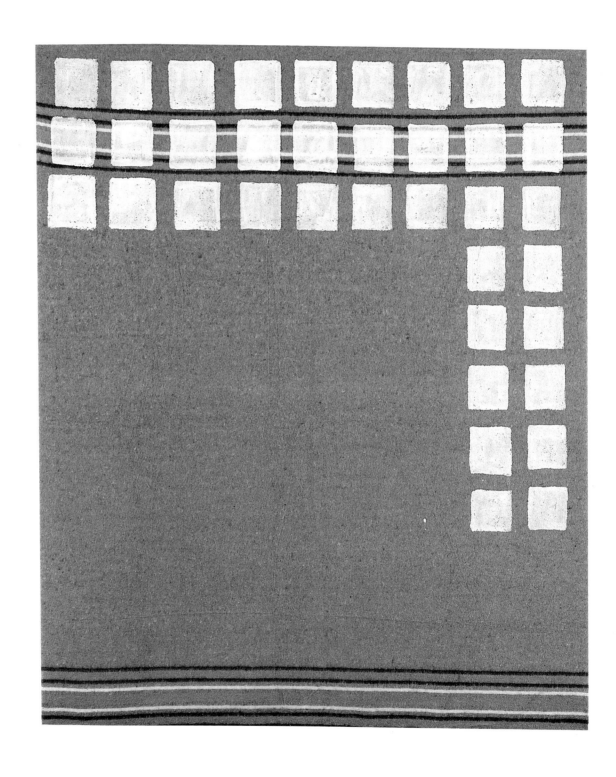

SIGMAR POLKE

71
Ich mach das schon Jess
1972
Oil on felt
124×112 (315×285)

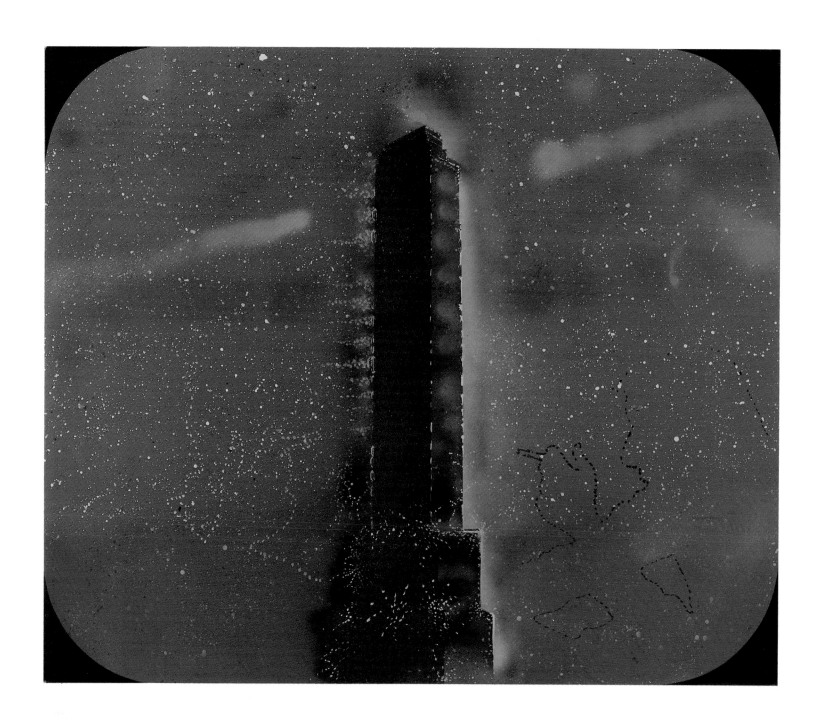

72
Zwei Köpfe
1971/73
Oil and cellulose on canvas
51×43 (130×110)

73
Skelett
1974
Dispersion on fabric
77×72 (196×183)

SIGMAR POLKE

74
Affen
1974
Dispersion and spray enamel on canvas
71 ×59 (180 ×150)

SIGMAR POLKE

75
Burda
1979/82
Dispersion on fabric
8 panels, Each: 35½×27½ (90×70)
Overall: 71×120¼ (180×305)

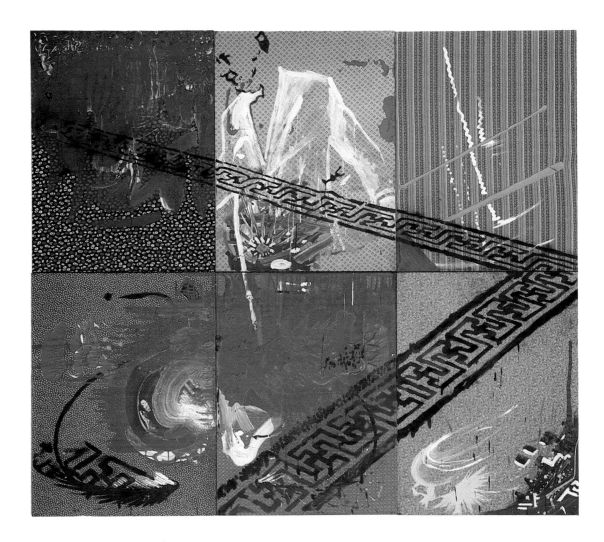

76
**Seit Benzin- und Heizölpreise fallen, wundert
mich nichts mehr**
1982
Dispersion on fabric
59 ×71 (150 ×180)

SIGMAR POLKE

77
Treppenhaus
1982
Dispersion on fabric
78³/₄ × 177 (200 × 450)

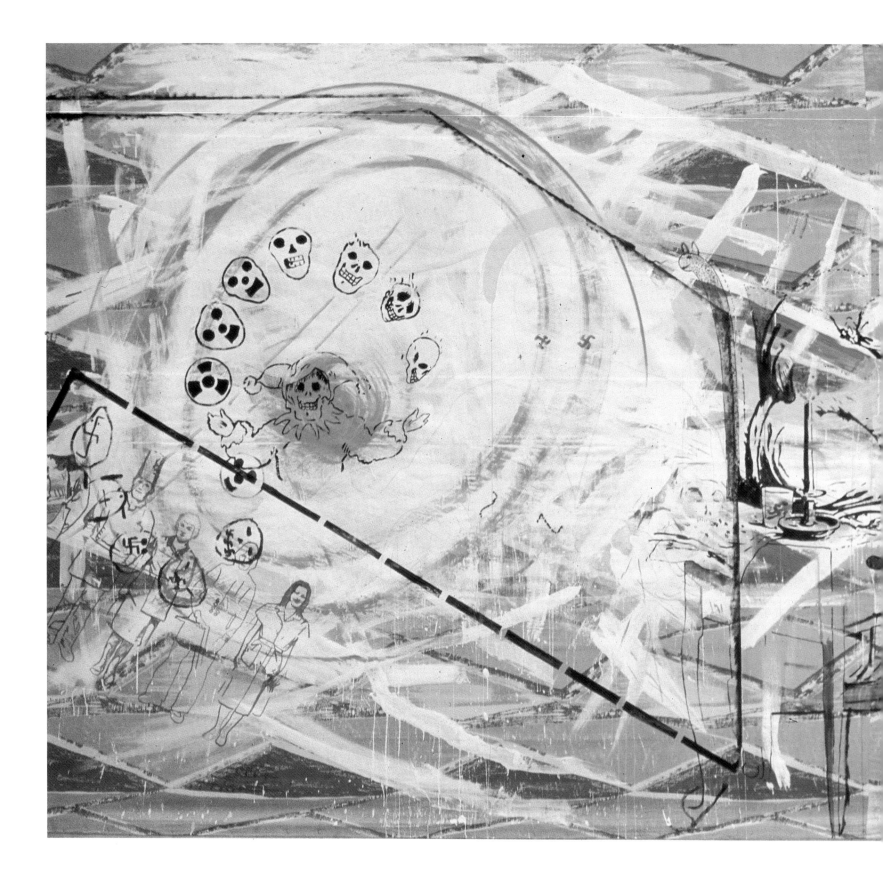

SIGMAR POLKE

78
Paganini
1982
Dispersion on canvas
78¾ × 177 (200 × 450)

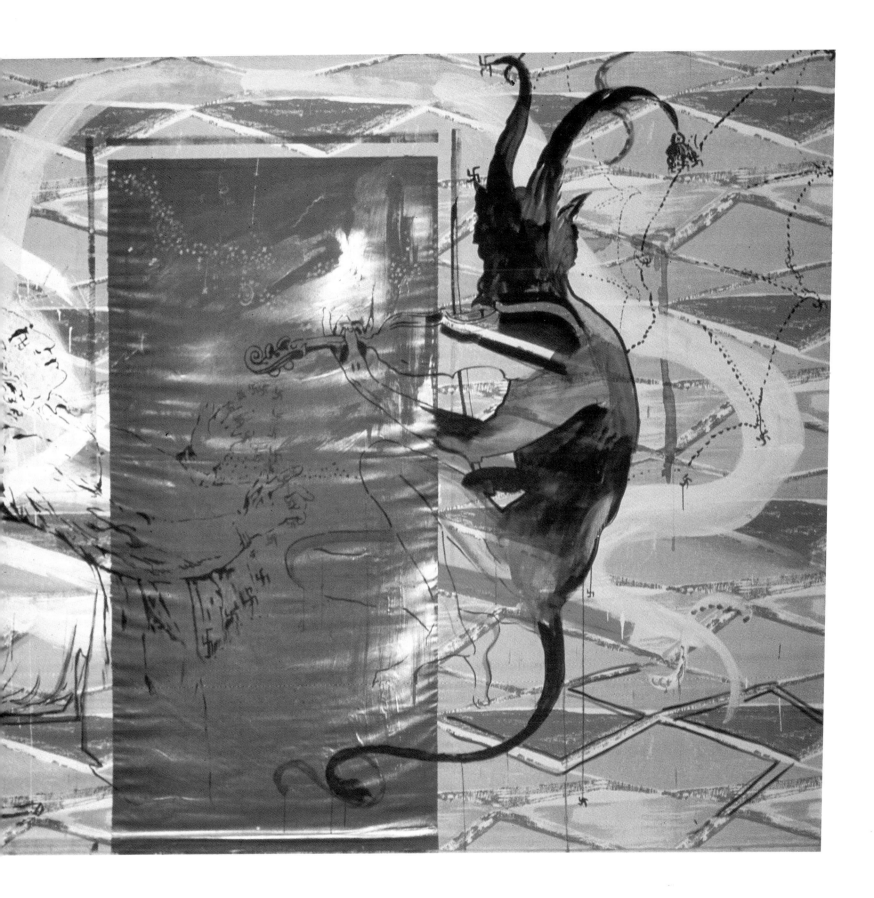

SIGMAR POLKE

79
Hannibal mit seinen Panzerelefanten
1982
Dispersion and lacquer on canvas
102½ × 79 (260 × 200)

SIGMAR POLKE

80
The Copyist
1982
Dispersion and lacquer on canvas
102½×79 (260×200)

JULIAN SCHNABEL

81
No. 17 (Red Cross Painting for N. Fisher 1978)
1977/78
Oil on canvas
96×48 (240×122)

JULIAN SCHNABEL

82
Accatone
1978
Oil on canvas
84 × 72 (210 × 180)

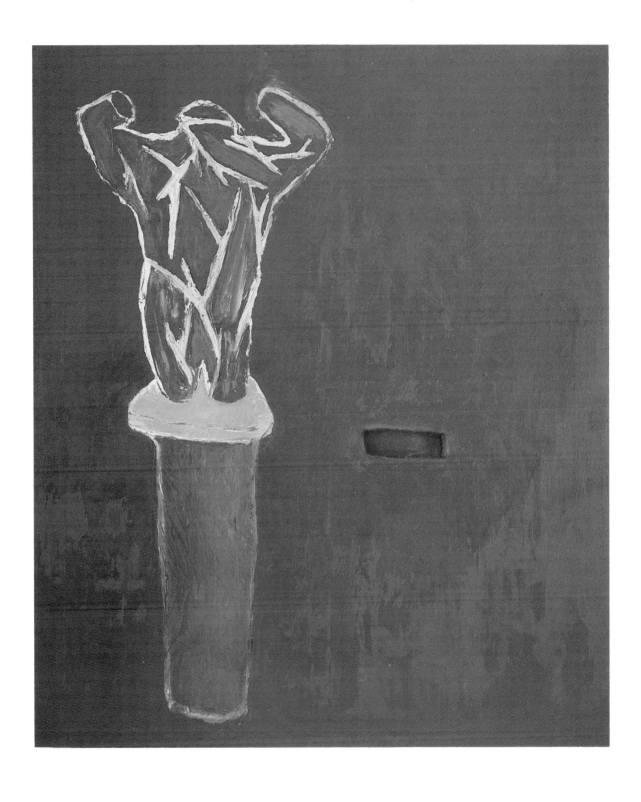

JULIAN SCHNABEL

83
The Death of Fashion
1978
Oil, crockery on canvas and wood
90×120×13 (225×300×32·5)

84
Divan
1978
Oil and crockery on wood
96 ×96 ×18 (240 ×240 ×45)

JULIAN SCHNABEL

85
Against Modernism (What to do with a corner in Madrid)
1979
Oil on canvas
96×96 (240×240)

JULIAN SCHNABEL

86
Insomnolent Brown Trimmed in Mink
1980
Oil on canvas
96×84 (240×210)

JULIAN SCHNABEL

87
Ornamental Despair (Painting for Ian Curtis)
1980
Oil on velvet
90×168 (228·6×426·7)

JULIAN SCHNABEL

88
Mr Bamboo Gets an X-ray
1980
Oil on velvet
90 × 168 (228·6 × 426·7)

JULIAN SCHNABEL

89
Bob's Worlds
1980
Oil, wax, crockery on wood and canvas
97½×146 (243·8×365·7)

JULIAN SCHNABEL

90
Starting to Sing: Artaud (3)
1981
Oil and rustoleum on canvas
168×156 (420×390)

91
Starting to Sing: Untitled (1)
1981
Oil and rustoleum on canvas
170×216 (425×540)

92
Starting to Sing: Florence Loeb (4)
1981
Oil and rustoleum on canvas
163×112 (407·5×280)

93
Starting to Sing: Untitled (2)
1981
Oil and rustoleum on canvas
166×228 (415×570)

90

91

92

93

JULIAN SCHNABEL

94
Fouffi-Nouti in Hell
1980
Oil on Chinese silk
91 ×85 (228 ×213)

JULIAN SCHNABEL

95
Aorta
1981
Oil on sisal rug with wooden frame
120×168 (300×420)

JULIAN SCHNABEL

96
Pre History: Glory, Honor, Privilege and Poverty
1981
Oil and antlers on pony skin
128×177 (324×450)

JULIAN SCHNABEL

97
Oar: For the one who comes out to know fear
1981
Oil, crockery, car body filler paste and wood on wood
127 × 175 × 13 (318 × 438 × 32·5)

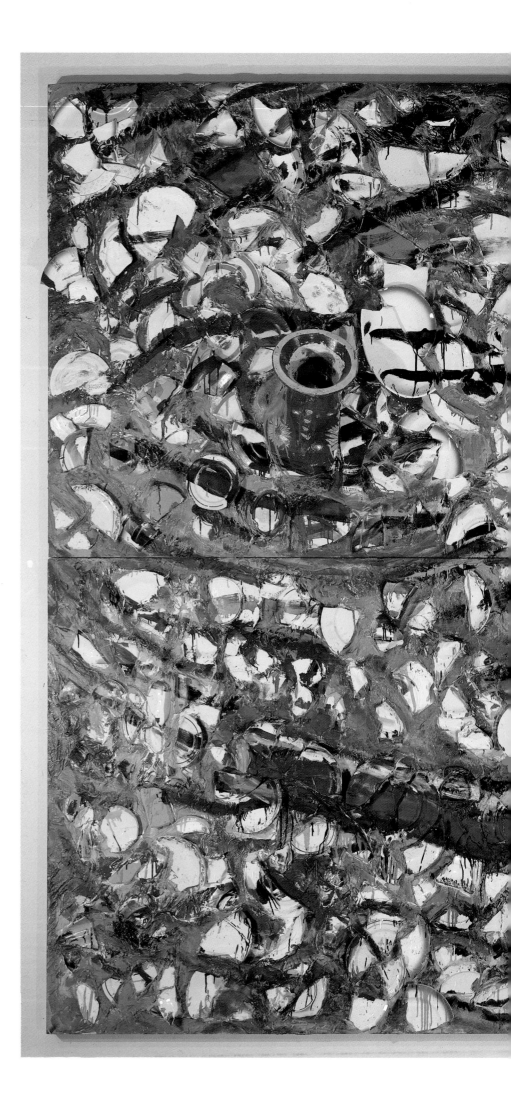

JULIAN SCHNABEL

98
Painting for Alan Moss
1981
Oil on jute
108×120 (270×300)

JULIAN SCHNABEL

99
The Sea
1981
Oil and crockery on wood
108 × 156 (274 × 390)

JULIAN SCHNABEL

100
Angela
1982
Oil on rug batting
132 × 60 (330 × 150)

JULIAN SCHNABEL

101
Olé
1982
Oil on tarpaulin
96 × 132 (277 × 335)

JULIAN SCHNABEL

102
Winter (Rose garden that Jacqueline built as a girl)
1982
Oil, crockery, antler, wood and bondo on wood
108×84 (270×210)

JULIAN SCHNABEL

103
Maria Callas, No. 4
1983
Oil on velvet
108×122 (274×305)

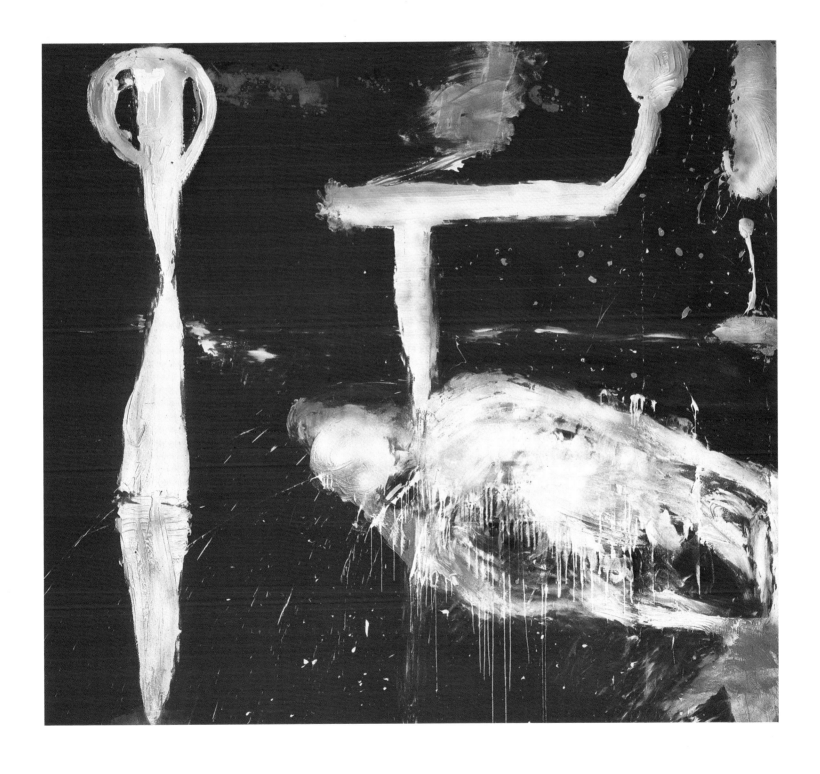

JULIAN SCHNABEL

104
Balzac
1983
Bronze
199 × 46 × 46 (497·5 × 115 × 115)

JULIAN SCHNABEL

105
Vito
1983
Bronze
108×28×27 (270×70×67·5)

JULIAN SCHNABEL

106
Memory and the Stimulus for Memory
1983
Oil and fibreglass on canvas
116×160 (290×400)

JULIAN SCHNABEL

107
A.D. (Wreath for Tennessee Williams)
1983
Oil and fibreglass on canvas
132×96 (335×244)